2017
Shari
Best w...
Thanks for the help -

Strategic Follow Up:

FIVE EASY STEPS TO BUILD YOUR BUSINESS

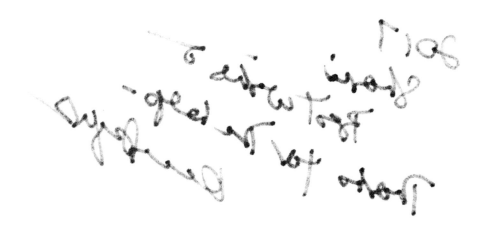

STRATEGIC FOLLOW UP
© 2017 Dr. Kaaren Douglas, All Rights Reserved.

ISBN: 978-0-9970083-0-2 (Print)
ISBN: 978-0-9970083-1-9 (E-Book)

Library of Congress Control Number: 2016920217
Douglas, Dr. Kaaren
Strategic Follow Up: Five easy steps to build your business/Dr. Kaaren Douglas

Medicus Publishing
107 N. Reino Rd. #181 • Newbury Park, CA 91320
info@medicuspublishing.com
www.medicuspublishing.com

MEDICUS PUBLISHING
107 N. Reino Rd. #181 • Newbury Park, CA 91320
info@ medicuspublishing.com
www.medicuspublishing.com

Strategic Follow Up:

FIVE EASY STEPS TO BUILD YOUR BUSINESS

**Dr. Kaaren Douglas,
The Follow Up Doctor**

Acknowledgments

ALTHOUGH I HAVE attempted to list many valuable resources and texts in the Appendix, I could not include all the sources I consulted to write this guide.

Valuable information and inspiration were contributed by Bob Burg, Joel Comm, Greg Spaulding, Mara Purl, Jason Williams, Carolyn Ruby, Remy Haynes, Dr. Bruce Kaplan, AJ Kahn, Roberta Nadler, Ellen Lubic, Kevin Hackenberg, Dr. Mary Watson, Bonnie Sharer, Neil Palache, Christopher Owen, Penny Francis, Karin Conway, Dr. Brian Grossman, Cheryl Smith & Nancy Halas, Douglas Byrd, and J. Christine McCray.

Many thanks are due my friends, clients, and contacts who I have been privileged to have in my life. Thanks also to my family and their continued support.

Copy Editing by Adrienne Moch.

Rebecca Finkel provided the cover design and Nick Zellinger developed my logo.

Contents

Disclaimer

THIS BOOK IS designed to provide information about the subject matter covered. It is sold with the understanding that the publisher and author are not engaged in rendering legal, accounting or other professional services. If legal or other expert assistance is required, the services of a competent professional should be sought.

It is not the purpose of this guide to reprint all the information that is otherwise available to business owners, but to complement, amplify and supplement other texts. For more information, see the many references in the Appendix.

Every effort has been made to make this book as complete and accurate as possible. However, there may be mistakes, both typographical and in content. Therefore, this text should be used as a general guide, and not as the ultimate source of follow-up information. Furthermore, this guide contains information on follow-up only up to the printing date.

The purpose of this guide is to educate and entertain. The author and Medicus Publishing shall have neither liability nor responsibility to any person or entity with respect to any loss or damage caused or alleged to be caused directly or indirectly by the information contained in this book.

If you do not wish to be bound by the above, you may return this book to the publisher for a full refund.

SECTION ONE

Chapter 1
Why Follow Up?

"The trouble with having an open mind, of course, is that people will insist on coming along and trying to put things in it."

Terry Pratchett (1948-2015),
author of fantasy novels

IMAGINE YOU GO to a networking mixer and meet:

- A distributor looking to recruit you to his business

- A professional networker you'd like to meet later for coffee

- A hypnotherapist who makes you laugh

- A lawyer who shoves a card into your hand and moves on

- A sexy real estate sales woman in soft clingy cashmere whose face is overshadowed by her ample cleavage

- A bored insurance salesman

- A chiropractor pushing nutritional products

- A marketing director from the local chamber who invites you to visit the chamber office

All of them give you their business cards, and some of them ask for yours.

Now what? Which, if any, of the people above would make-sense for you to contact after the event?

We collect business cards, take them home and toss them on the desk. Then we go to the next event without ever deciding what to do with the cards we just got.

Is this you? Are you overwhelmed and don't know what to do with the business cards you collect? That is the OLD way of doing business. I suggest that for networking to be productive, you must be proactive. You must have a plan, and commit to interacting with people for a long time.

When you are at an event, or interacting with people on social media, do you sift and sort the contacts you make on the spot?

What criteria are you using to decide which are the best people for you to talk with again?

With a limited amount of time, how do you target the time you spend on follow-up to keep in touch with the best contacts for **you**?

Despite thinking you are in the business of "selling" your product or service, the truth is you are in the business of building and sustaining relationships. That is the NEW way of doing business. That takes effort, a kind of effort most people don't understand or spend much time on.

As you network in person or online, you will meet people who become your customers or clients, and those you want as friends. And best of all, you will find raving fans who help you grow your business.

Does follow-up work to build business?

- **Mike W.** was selling doors and windows. One holiday season, he sent out 50 holiday cards to former customers just wishing them well. No sales pitch was included. He received a call from one of the customers who told him how happy she was to hear from him, as she had lost his information. She invited him over to look at a new job at her home. At the time of the sales presentation, he was able to generate $10,000 in new business from that one customer.

- **Another salesperson** noted she built her online business in Germany by using personal messages on Facebook.

- **Roberta N.** posted on Facebook: "Just got a call from a past client who saved my card for 10 years! She had a referral. A clear message: follow up! Always stay in touch!"

- **A husband and wife** built their online business by consistently following up, along with having an accountability partner who they talk to every day.

- **Karen B** stated: "As a real estate broker, I understand the importance of follow-up. However, sometimes in our busy worlds, if we don't have some type of system set up to keep that follow-up consistent, time goes by and it feels awkward to reconnect with the person. In a training session I did with several agents, this was exactly the discussion. I challenged everyone to take the time to write a personal, i.e., handwritten letter to those who they had been out of contact with to apologize for not having been in contact recently and offering to meet with them for coffee or lunch to catch up. The results were outstanding. Every one of the agents had at least one person contact them saying it was good to hear from them, several set up lunches with numerous past clients, and one resulted in a sale from a referral they got from one of the past clients for $18,000! Follow-up is the key to any business but most importantly consistent followup leads to success!"

- **An Australian beach boy entrepreneur** sends cards to those who buy from him on eBay and to those he meets in business. He admits he does not do the phone follow-up he could do, but because he consistently sends so many cards, he always has someone calling him.

- **A mortgage broker in Toronto** found sending heartfelt cards has generated new mortgage business.

- **Robert Shemin,** well-known author and entrepreneur, posted on Facebook: "Persistence is a key to success. This guy is selling illegal poorly copied versions of my book in the streets of Medellin. He still kept trying to close the sale even after my assistant and I told him repeatedly that I wrote the book. Stay focused on your goal and do not give up. I bought from him."

We have entered a new phase in business, with more ways to communicate, and new expectations about what it means to have a career in business. You may be feeling overwhelmed, without a clear way to proceed. Imagine you can create a new way that will be more effective and ensure meaningful connections that last.

In this book, I suggest ways for you to put together a system that works for you. It will use old standby tools, like face-toface connection, as well as more effective use of the digital tools you may know about, but may not be using in the most effective way.

At the end of the day, you want to make sure a prospective customer, client or business partner (if you are in a network marketing business) decides to get to know you better, and becomes a life-long customer and fan. You need to meet and follow up with a lot of people to achieve that goal, but the journey can be fun, and the results are impressive when you do it right.

Chapter 2
Trust Me, I'm a Doctor.

"Observe, record, tabulate, communicate…know that by practice alone you can become expert."

William Osler (1849-1919),
father of modern medicine

YOU AND I AGREE follow-up is important to build your business. It has been critical to me, as over my lifetime, I have kept in touch with family and friends all over the world.

How did I go from being in a full-time medical practice and an academic position to becoming The Follow Up Doctor? It may seem to be a total disconnect, but it has been a natural transition.

Let me explain.

As part of a nuclear family, I learned how to "follow up" and keep in touch at a young age. I was fortunate to have a large extended family, and wonderful grandparents and great grandparents with whom I spent my summers. Then I went back to my parents, wherever we were living at the time, to start the new school year.

Before going home at the end of the summer one year, Great Grandma Rose advised me about letter writing. "Don't just say 'I love you.' Tell me what you have been doing. Tell me about your family, and about school," she said. She told me to say something interesting, and keep writing letters.

In those days, a letter cost pennies to send, and a long-distance phone call was rare and expensive. We only saw the grandparents

and my mom's extended family in the summer. And my great grandmother and I were close. She wanted to hear about my daily life when I went home.

From then on, I was a letter writer. I wrote to my family, and friends I left behind as I moved around the States and Europe. My college roommate and I are still in touch, largely because I sent her cards and letters over the years. She told me, "I'm glad you kept writing, because I'm so bad at it." I knew I wanted to keep people I met in my life, and I accepted the responsibility for making it happen. I am a **Follow-up Expert** and an innovator who has always embraced new ways to do things, as well as technologies as they became available.

Subsequent to residency training, I opened a solo family practice where I supervised multiple employees, and ran my office. Before opening the practice, I attended a workshop to learn ways to schedule and chart. My practice was so efficient, I was able to build and maintain it with only one receptionist/bookkeeper, one nurse, and one assistant. When it came time for me to go back to graduate school, I was able to sell the practice to the hospital.

Part of the reason the hospital was interested in buying my practice was because my charts were legible. In the patient records, I used check-off forms with short comments, a predecessor to computerized records, instead of handwritten notes. Lengthier records, such as descriptions of physical examinations, and notes about hospitalized patients, were dictated and transcribed. And my secretary was one of the first in town to have a personal computer to track records and billing.

As a result of my postdoctoral studies, I received a master's of science in public health. I held multiple academic positions in Kansas City, MO and Irvine, CA. Along the way, I taught medical students, family practice and internal medicine resident physicians, and geriatric fellows. I managed a group of faculty, fulfilled my own faculty responsibilities, wrote and published a textbook, and maintained a medical practice.

Moving from academic medicine into the private sector, I became a physician administrator in a not-for-profit corporation. I had a contract and accomplished the goals set for me in record time. Unfortunately, my husband was diagnosed with terminal cancer at the same time huge cuts occurred where I worked. It allowed me the freedom to be at home with my husband. Eventually it led me to cast about for a different way to contribute. It allowed me to start my own business, and to help people in an entirely different way.

Trust Me, I'm A Doctor

The Follow Up Doctor

Now I am **The Follow Up Doctor.** I apply what I learned from being a clinician and teacher to working with clients.I mentor them on how to manage overwhelm, and help them develop a follow-up system tailored to their needs.

Before World War II, most families stayed put. Since then, our society has been increasingly mobile, as the men coming back from the war took advantage of the GI Bill to get an education, or moved somewhere they could use the skills they had acquired in military service.

When I was a kid, our family moved a lot. I had to learn how to meet people and try to fit in at a young age. I was forced to develop social skills to cope at new schools and new churches every couple years. We lived in California, Alaska, Washington, Colorado, Texas, and South Dakota. Finally landed back in Colorado, but my moves were not over. When I was a junior in high school, my dad was fired when he and his professional colleagues tried to form a union at the company where he worked. My family could no longer afford the tuition of the college preparatory school I attended, so I finished high school at a public school, knowing no one, and drawing again on my resilience to get along in a new environment.

Meeting new people in business is similar to what I learned as a young person. When I first started going from one networking opportunity to the next, I read Bob Burg's book, *Endless Referrals*. His recommendations resonated with me. He advised sending personalized thank you note cards to people I met at networking events. He suggested letting them know I'd like to help them if I could. As a result of following his sage advice, I built upon the fol-low-up habits I had cultivated to keep in touch with friends I met along the way.

When I work with clients, I tell them: "Don't wait for anyone to follow up with you. More than likely they won't. Take the responsibility on yourself to make it happen."

As Tony Robbins, author and life strategist says: "Anyony who is able to consistently achieve success has a strategy." Think of me as your **Follow-Up Strategist**.

I have had a network marketing business since 2001. I am guessing I have experienced similar challenges to those you face, as a solopreneur, or owner of a home-based business. I can teach you how to persevere as well.

You may need to get out of your comfort zone, and use some forms of communication that are new to you. I attribute my success in follow-up to the fact that I am always in front of the crowd, experimenting with new technologies.

As communication options appeared, I started using them. First it was email, then cell phones, My Space, video email, Facebook, Twitter, LinkedIn, Skype, Instagram and Pinterest. When I think about all the ways I keep in touch, it feels like skiing downhill, going faster and faster with new twists and turns as I add on more and more social media. I'm always looking for better ways to keep in touch. And so are your prospects, customers and clients. You must stay ahead of them. Be a leader.

And, oh yes, I still send greeting cards and letters. Now it helps me stand out, because so few people send mail.

Chapter 3
Develop Good Habits

"Your beliefs become your thoughts,
Your thoughts become your words,
Your words become your actions,
Your actions become your habits,
Your habits become your values,
Your values become your destiny."

Mahatma Gandhi (1869-1948),
Indian leader, proponent of nonviolent disobedience

Good habits help you grow your business. They help you reach your goals because you are repeating the behaviors that generate income. The first step to creating good habits is to recognize the behavior you want to do repeatedly. If eventually you are able to delegate part of what you do, you need to be able to explain to someone else exactly what you do.

If I were to ask you now to describe the process you go through after you meet someone, what would you say?

If you are like me, it might take a little soul-searching to identify the steps you take. Before I developed an improved system for myself, I first looked at what I was already doing, to see if I could make it easier or more efficient.

Eventually I wanted to be able to delegate whatever part of the process I could to a virtual assistant. For that to happen, I would need to be able to show them what part of the process they could do to help me. I needed to know what I could turn over to someone else, and what I absolutely must do myself.

In addition, I realized I had to develop a routine and habit of follow-up, so I knew what was working. I had to make sure I was in touch with prospects on a regular basis. The key here was "develop a routine and habit."

Sometimes we think of habits in a negative way; for example, I have a habit of watching TV when I prepare and eat my meals. All the diet books say I should focus on eating, and do nothing else at the same time, but I like the entertainment value of watching a movie or other show. This is a perfect example of what could be seen as a "bad" habit, but one I am not planning on changing anytime soon.

We can choose what habits to keep or develop to make sure we get things done. For example, after I feed my animals in the morning, I go for a walk with them. By all accounts, this is a "good" habit.

You have heard the expression, "I am a creature of habit." All of us can develop habits that save us time and make us more efficient. Can you think of habits you currently have that fall into this category?

For example, when you get up in the morning, do you have the habit of exercising before you take a shower and get ready for your day? Are there other things you do that make your day move along more smoothly? When we habitually do something, it saves us time because we don't have to think about it. We just do it. The way to develop a positive habit involves repeating a learned behavior over and over in the same way and for a particular length of time. Most references say we need hree weeks to develop a habit, and then we are able to do the behavior almost unconsciously.

If you have tried to develop a good habit, and found you were not successful, you may not have been ready.

Five Stages of Readiness
1. Pre-contemplation: Do not see a need.
2. Contemplation: Not ready to take action.
3. Preparation: Setting the stage.
4. Action: Hurrah.
5. Maintenance: The behavior has become a habit.

If you jump into action without being ready, you may not be able to stay motivated long enough to form a new habit that can keep you in action. Or you may not be ready because you really don't know how to proceed.

Once you realize you need to do things differently, and developing a habit is your goal, there is another process involved before you can take sustained action. This involves learning a new behavior. To do that you must go through multiple stages.

I love to dance, and I have gotten good enough to compete at it. But I wasn't always that skilled. I had to learn how to perform the dance moves, and that took time and effort.

For example, to dance a tango effortlessly, I first had to learn the steps, and how to follow the leader I danced with. I recognized initially that I didn't know the steps, but I had the desire to learn them. Then I went to classes, and took private lessons to learn the steps and how to follow the male dancer I was dancing with.

Because I was learning to dance competitively, I also had to learn how to do the routines shadow dancing (solo with my arms up, as if I were dancing with a male dancer). Then I practiced,

practiced, practiced, putting together the steps I learned with feel-ing the lead of the man I was dancing with. And I went to compe-titions and danced with my teacher in front of an audience. All the time my skill was improving. When I dance the tango now, it is at an unconscious level. I just listen to the music, and enjoy the dance.

Habitual behavior is performed at the "4th stage of learning." What does that mean, and why is it important? Let me explain.

Dr. Thomas Gordon, a clinical psychologist, described what it takes to develop competence at the unconscious level in **The Four Stages of Learning** model. According to Dr. Gordon, it takes at least three weeks of consistent effort to make a behavior a habit, because you need to move through these learning stages. As you are learning a skill, like dancing the tango, you move from conscious incompetence, to skill acquisition, to conscious use of the new skill, and as the skill becomes a habit, unconscious use of it. I moved from not knowing the tango steps at all, to learning the steps without a partner, then consciously dancing the steps with different partners, and with practice to the point it became automatic, being able to dance the tango with almost any partner without thinking about it.

In the world of networking and follow-up, when you were starting out with your business and starting to go to networking events, you may have gotten lots of business cards, but had no consistent way to deal with them. You were at the first stage of learning: **Unconscious Incompetent**. You didn't yet see the behavior as something that needed to change.

At some point, you got overwhelmed by all the contacts you were making, and realized you are not sure what to do with all the business cards from networking events. You were at the second stage: **Conscious Incompetent**. This is where many of my clients are when I meet them.

One of the first things I do is introduce clients to *ScanBizCards*, a smartphone app. They learn how to use it and start to scan new business cards immediately after they get them. This puts them at the third stage: Conscious Competence.

After about three weeks of consistently using the app, they have formed a new habit. At that point, they are in stage four, Unconscious Competent, otherwise referred to as the 4th Level of Competence, because they no longer wonder what to do with the business cards.

They just scan them, send their contacts a quick email and are done. The contacts are in their database and ready to go.

It doesn't matter what behavior you work on; as you try something new, you go through these four learning stages. To be better at follow-up, you need to look at what you are currently doing, and what needs to change to make your follow-up more consistent. But, to keep from being overwhelmed and increase the likelihood that a behavior will become a habit, choose only one behavior at a time to work on. For me, I'm going to grab something to eat, watch the next episode of "Murdoch Mysteries," and think about what habit I should work on next.

Chapter 4
Evaluate Your System

"Being busy does not always mean real work. The object of all work is production or accomplishment and to either of these ends there must be forethought, system, planning, intelligence, and honest purpose, as well as perspiration. Seeming to do is not doing."

**Thomas A. Edison (1847-1931),
inventor and businessman**

How EFFECTIVELY do you follow up?

Whenever I present at a workshop, or speak to a local Chamber of Commerce, or other groups, I ask participants a series of questions about follow-up. This test alerts them to options they may not have thought of. I provide it here so you can think about what you are doing well, and think about ways you could improve. All these ideas are great benchmarks to measure against as you build your business.

Rate yourself on a scale of 0 to 5, where 0 is not true, and 5 is very true.

- Each time I meet a new person, I put their information into my cell phone or contact manager

immediately, or at least within 48 hours.

- I make sure I meet and add a new person to my contact manager every week.

- I communicate in some way with each new contact no later than 48 hours after meeting them.

- I keep track of events that matter to people in my network, and send them a card, an email or a message to acknowledge the events.

- I make notes every time I interact with someone, or attempt to contact them in any way.

- I take note of gifts a person might appreciate.

- I keep my contacts aware of what is happening in my professional life, including address or

business changes.

- When people ask, I can refer them to needed resources.

- I have a Board of Advisors I can call if I need help, information or a resource.

> Maximum score is 45.
> 40 to 45 Superstar potential
> 31 to 40 Off to a great start
> 21 to 30 Doing some things right
> 0 to 20 Time to change

How did you do? Are you a master of follow-up yet?

Sometimes participants in workshops or presentations are reluctant to commit to answers, and don't write down their responses. They do themselves a disservice, because all of us need to be conscious of our behaviors so we can choose to change them if we need to.

The upside of writing down what you are doing today is that it gives you a starting point to measure improvement. The vast majorities of participants, who take the test, score less than 30, and recognize they need to improve by adding something to what they are currently doing. Only once did I have a participant score in the Superstar category, and she is a Realtor whose follow-up is better than anyone else I know.

When I meet with someone I am getting to know, I use a series of questions to learn more about them, and to pique their interest about things they may not have thought about. (See Appendix.)

Questions you can now ask yourself:

- How often do I currently follow up after I meet someone?

- Do I ask my contacts what their preferred method of follow-up is, and then tailor how I follow up to their preference?

- How often do I make more than three contacts after meeting a prospect or talking to them the first time? This includes all forms of contact, e.g. phone, email, text, Facebook, LinkedIn, Twitter, card or letter.

- Do I want to be better than the average at follow- up?

To get what other people don't have, you have to do what other people won't do.

Become really good at follow-up, and your current and potential customers and clients will remember you when they need to buy your product or service.

Recently, the handle to my front door came off in my hands. I needed a locksmith to repair the door *that day,* and knew I had met a couple locksmiths over the years at the different networking events I had attended. But none of them had followed up with me. As a result, I did what most of us would do; I went to the Internet and looked for a local locksmith with good reviews on *Yelp*.

Since the locksmiths I had met never kept in touch with me, I had to go online to find someone who could fix my door. If you don't keep in touch with your contacts, they won't remember you and how to get in touch with you when they need your services. They will go to the Internet to find someone. That person may not be you, but your competition instead.

You never know when someone might need your services. What if the person who serviced your furnace or garage door, or installed your new windows, never kept in touch with you? You might not remember their name the next time you needed their service, or when a friend or colleague asked you for a referral for their service or product. How would you find them again? So, how will your prospects know to contact you?

Recently a man who had just taken a job locally and wanted to get health insurance for his family requested a referral to someone selling health insurance. He had moved here from India, and his son was slated to start school in a month. After he found a home for the family, his wife and son were joining him. He did not have an insurance benefit where he worked, and he wanted to be all set for when they got here.

Although I have a large network, including many insurance agents and brokers, NONE of them have kept in touch with me. I wanted to give my contact several names, so he could pick whom he wanted to buy from. I posted on Facebook, and asked agents to contact me directly so I could pass on their information.

This is a redacted version of the responses I got:

The first comment was from RS who recommended DJ through Givesurance, where a portion of the agent's commission went to the charity she worked with. DJ responded.

MS replied to the post, and recommended another agent, CK, an agent I knew.

I responded to CK requesting her up-to-date contact info to pass on to my referral.

DF posted: "My husband SF can help."

I responded: Thanks to everyone. Please pass on to the folks you mentioned that they should contact me. The money is in the follow up.

RN responded: Awesome thread!!!

I responded, " So far I've been contacted by one person . I will pass on his info to my contact."

DF responded again about her husband. I replied to her, "… just have him message me. " [Her husband never contacted me directly.]

MK responded: "You're absolutely right, had this been my field of expertise I would have been all over this.

JJ responded with the name of TK: "He is a wonderful and attentive health insurance agent."

TK replied to her post: "Thank you, Dr. J!!" [Although I had asked that agents contact me directly, this agent complimented the person recommending him, and never messaged me.]

I replied to posts: Ok. So I have had 2 agents I know respond to this thread . I have told my referral that I will give him the names of several people. I am still waiting for agents that I already know to contact me. Thanks to DJ and CK (the only agents who contacted me privately with their contact information).

JJ replied: Kaaren Douglas, you can keep waiting on the ones who are non-responsive, or you can go forward to the few who are!

I replied: "Thanks JJ. I wanted to make sure I gave them a real chance, since my original post was on Sunday.

In the end, only two agents contacted me directly as I requested. I knew both of them, and I gave both their names and contact information via email to the person who had requested the referral.

Your contacts won't remember how to get in touch with you when they need you unless you follow up with them and keep doing it long term. Yes, even after they have become your customers. In the long run, it is easier to sell again to someone who has already bought from you, but only if you keep in touch. Otherwise, that next sale might go to one of your competitors.

The OLD way of doing business is to "hound" contacts until they "buy or die." The NEW way is to strive to develop real relationships with people you meet.

Many people are using consultants to help them post on social media as a way to market to potential contacts, but are not making meaningful connections through their digital tools. If you recognize that only a tiny percentage of the people you are connected with on social media ever see anything you post, you will see some of the disadvantages of a disorganized, unplanned approach to follow-up. In addition, it can be expensive, if you are paying someone to manage your digital assets for you.

In Chapter 5, I outline the *Five Easy Steps* I have developed for Strategic Follow Up. It is a new and complete system that you can integrate into what you are already doing well. The following chapters describe in detail what you need to know to implement the steps. They will take you from chaos and overwhelm to organization and increased business success. You will be developing your own system based on what you already do well, adding the suggestions from the Five Easy Steps.

As you develop your system, commit to improving it by changing just one thing at a time. Practice that one new behavior in addition to whatever else you are doing for at least three weeks, so it is embedded in your routine. Then tackle the next behavior, and do the same thing. Over time, the new additions to your system will become habit, and follow-up will become automatic.

Tidbits About Follow-Up

- 48% of salespeople never follow up with people they meet.
- 10% of salespeople get back to people they meet three times or more.
- 80% of sales are made on the 5th to 12th contact.
- For every 100 people you meet, if you refer business to each of them, five become life-long customers.
- For every 100 people you meet, if you stay in touch with them, six become lifelong customers.

SECTION TWO

Chapter 5
The Five Easy Steps

"The secret of getting ahead is getting started."

Mark Twain (Samuel Longhorn Clemens 1835-1910), author and humorist

THE BEST FOLLOW-UP SYSTEM is the one you use. After taking the self-test in Chapter 4, you have a better idea about what you are already doing well.

Over the years, I have been building my list of 5,000+ contacts, and have developed the **Five Easy Steps**. I call them the **Five Easy Steps to Build Your Business**, because I believe effective follow-up is critical to growing a business.

This guide details the follow-up system I use. It is a step-by-step exploration of the system I developed over the years to build and maintain a network of business contacts, customers, and friends.

Within the steps, there are certain essential actions you need to do to be effective at follow-up. As you become more proficient in using the steps, they will become habits. When they become automatic, you will be amazed how easily you are building and using a data base, and your time will be more productive. Keep in mind, it is more cost-effective to put people into your contact manager and stay in touch with them than it is to go to meetings and never follow up with the contacts you make.

The next five chapters describe in detail how to do each one of the steps. Chapter 11 describes why and how to keep in touch with people after they have decided to do business with you. Please, don't falter at this point. You always want your customers to know how important they are to you. It is always cheaper to keep a customer happy than it is to find new ones. Customers also can be a powerful resource for you when they become your fans, and help you build your business with referrals.

The Five Easy Steps For Strategic Follow-up Are:
1. Sift and Sort
2. Keep Track
3. Speak Their Language
4. Say It Right
5. Follow Up Every Day

Chapter 6
Step One: Sift and Sort

"For sure, …people have access to more information now than any other people who have ever lived on earth. And I think we do a pretty good job of sorting out what's important."

**Bob Schieffer,
television journalist**

As you collect business cards at the events you attend, it is helpful to put the people you meet into groups for future follow-up. Since you will invest a lot of time following up with these people, you want to choose wisely.

Before you attend any event, ask yourself:

- Do you have a plan of action?

- What do you know about the sponsoring organization?

- Can you volunteer to raise your profile with the attendees and organizers?

- Who are the most likely attendees?

- Are there people who belong to specific business categories that you would like to meet?

- Can you research people you want to meet online, and familiarize yourself with how they look to be able to find them?

- Have you identified contacts who will help you the most?

- Have you written out a commercial appropriate for the group?

- Have you practiced what you will say, so it sounds natural?
- Do you have a way of recording someone's contact information if they do not have a business card to give you?

As you mingle with other attendees, seek out people you don't know, and those who seem to attract others. This ensures you meet some new people, and maybe some who can introduce you to others in the room.

If you have specific people or members of specific business sections you want to meet, make the most of your time by spending it getting to know them. As I will go into in more detail, this is the only way to decide if they are someone you can enjoy connecting with long term.

Ask people you meet to introduce you to others you would like to meet. As an ambassador for a local Chamber of Commerce, I loved meeting new attendees, and introducing them to people who would be interested in their business. You can do the same.

If you are nervous meeting new people, focus on others rather than yourself. Act *as if* you are an ambassador for the group, find out who people want to meet and make the introductions. Eleanor Roosevelt wrote about being devastated by fear and self-consciousness. She fought and conquered her anxiety by helping people who were worse off than she was. Model yourself after her, and make it a goal to help others you meet however you can.

Know what you want to say about yourself, and your business, and know what you are going to ask the people you meet. Remember you are sorting to see if you would like to meet with them again.

Only ask for a business card if you have had a chance to talk to an individual long enough to decide if you can put them into a group. This is not the same thing as prejudging merely on the basis of how someone looks, or other potential superficial characteristics.

For example, Malcolm Gladwell interviewed Bob Golomb, master car salesman, about how he is able to sell on average more than double what the typical car salesman sells. Golomb revealed that he tries to look for traits like confidence, and knowledge, and gives everyone the benefit of the doubt. He does not prejudge people who come into the dealership solely on appearance.

My parents had a friend, John, in the sports car club they belonged to, who was interested in getting one of the original Mercedes-Benz gullwing coupes. John went to the Mercedes dealership showroom in his usual attire: sloppy casual khaki slacks, and wrinkled shirt and jacket. He shuffled in, stoop shouldered, looking suspiciously like a bum who had come in off the street.

An older salesman sized up this poorly dressed gray-haired man, and told a young salesman to take care of him. When the young man approached him, John said he was interested in driving the car. So the young man and he took a test drive. At its conclusion, John told the young salesman he would be back. The next day, he returned to the dealership showroom, and the young man greeted him cordially. John declared he wanted to buy the car he had driven, and when the young salesman asked how he would like to pay for it, John said he was paying in cash.

Master the Art of Conversation

Although I am telling you to sort the people you meet into categories, I want to emphasize that before you decide where they fit, you must have a conversation with them. Selling cars and networking are not the same thing, but Golomb knew how to listen, and mastered the art of picking up on subtleties that helped him sort out his potential customers.

Be like Golomb. Try to find out as much as possible about people you meet. What do you have in common? Are they someone you want to talk to again?

What kinds of questions will help you make that decision? Try asking:

- How did you get started in your business?
- What do you like most about your business?
- What kinds of referrals are you looking for?
- How do you like [the organization sponsoring the event]?
- Who are you looking to meet?
- What do you do for fun?
- How can I help you, e.g. introduce you to someone here?

When I go to events I do my best to sort through the cards I collect on the spot. And I don't ask for a card or follow up with anyone I don't feel is a good fit for me.

How can you tell if someone you meet isn't a good fit for you?

- What does their body language tell you about them? Is there a lack of eye contact?

- When you are conversing with them, does the conversation feel off? Are they interrupting you to tell you about their products or services?

- Do you feel like moving backward to get away from them? Listen to that feeling, and run the other way.

- After you have encouraged them to tell you about themselves, are they interested in learning more about you? If not, what does that tell you?

- Are they pushing their business card in your face, but not interested in getting yours?

The most important criterion I use when I meet new people is to decide if we have rapport, because people are more likely to want to work with people they like.

As Gertrude Stein said, "I like familiarity. In me it does not breed contempt. Only more familiarity."

> **Rapport: An environment of trust, in which both people can express ideas. How do you know if you have rapport with someone you've just met?**
> - Are you getting eye contact?
> - Is their body language similar to yours?
> - Is your conversation on pace?
> - Does it "feel right"?
> - Do you enjoy talking to them?

Once you know you have rapport, decide if you would like to have this person as a customer. Would you like working with them? Could you help each other? Is this someone you would like as a friend?

In workshops I present on this topic, I find participants recognize rapport, and know when they have found someone they like. But this is where they stop. They don't seem to be able to take their sorting further. To date, no one at the workshops has had a system for deciding whom to follow up with. Nobody puts their contacts into distinct categories.

Until I realized sorting people into categories makes it easier to follow up with the best contacts for me, I was overwhelmed too. Now I decide on the spot, and put them into three simple categories. I just put an A, B or C on the business card, and implement follow up based on which category the person fits into.

Sort Into Categories:

- **A** for **Absolute best client or customer.** Someone you like who needs your product or service, can afford to buy from you, and is authorized to purchase. You may need a longer conversation to confirm these criteria before following up long term.

- **B** for **Beneficial business partner.** Someone who may not need your product or service, but has similar customers or clients to yours. You might be able to refer to each other for mutual benefit.

- **C** for **Contact long term.** You don't see them as possible customers, or working business partners, but you would like to socialize with them as friends. I also put individuals in this category who have a Circle of Influence and value networking like I do. (See Create a Board of Advisors)

If someone doesn't fall into a category, you don't need to keep their business card, or feel obligated to follow up with them. If you meet them at another networking event, or you connect with them through social media because of a shared interest, you can reevaluate your decision at that time. If they fit into a category at that point, feel free to follow up with them.

At each event, collect cards from people you see as possible customers (*Category A*). In addition to the Category A cards, you may want to collect cards from at least one or two people at the event who can give you referrals once they get to know you (*Category B*). You can think of these individuals as part of your long term m arketing plan. In my experience, when you meet someone you want to be friends with, that is a bonus (*Category C*).

Make notes on the business cards as you get them, or put information into your smartphone. If you have *Evernote* or *CamScanner*, you can make notes about the people you meet, as well as scan their business cards on the spot.

There is a new application available for the iPhone, called *Lincsphere*. It allows you to connect at events with people who are also using the app, as well as track your contacts with them. Keep it in mind, as it will do much of what I suggest.

After you have five cards total from possible customers or business partners, you can leave the event. Why quit with only five cards? Because the number of times you contact individuals adds up geometrically. It is better to strive for five contacts that you know you want to follow up with versus getting 10-20 business cards and not following up with any of them, because either they are not a good fit for you, or you are trapped in overwhelm.

Create a Board of Advisors

Are you meeting people who have skills and knowledge that could be helpful to you? Perhaps their knowledge and connections are much broader than the business they talk about most of the time. Because of their networks, they can be a resource for you or your contacts.

Think of them as your personal Mastermind Group. One criterion for membership in your Board of Advisors is that they are accessible when you need help sorting through a problem. These are a few of my personal advisors.

Neil Palache, The Wealth Creator Company for Women. When I need advice about investments, or management of property, or information about financial services, he is the person I talk to. Neil is a master networker and a terrific resource for a variety of services.

Mike Weissenborn, Sales Manager, Granite Transformations, has helped me in the past with installation of doors and windows in my home. He is very knowledgeable about contractors, and if I need a service, I call for his advice.

Carol Singer Haaz, Southern California Realtor. Carol wrote *Don't Be a Secret Agent.* She is masterful at marketing and follow-up, and has given me some great ideas for innovative ways to brand myself.

Roberta Nadler, Connect the Dots Advertising. Roberta is an expert on marketing and promotional products and programs. She is always surprising me with innovative ideas.

Who among your contacts could you invite to be on your *Board of Advisors*? Who do you know that has a large circle of influence? Write down their names, and keep your eyes open as you meet new people. Would they be someone you could ask for a resource or help you solve a problem? When you find these people, let them know how much you appreciate them and their help.

> **Tips for Success:**
> 1. Carry business cards with you, no matter where you are going.
> 2. Meet five new people at every event.
> 3. Schedule follow-up meetings on the spot.

Action Steps I Will Take Now:

- Prepare for the next event I attend by researching the organization and the likely attendees to decide who I want to meet.

- Make sure I have business cards and flyers about my business to take with me to the next event.

- At any event, write an A, B, or C on the front of business cards before scanning them.

- Feel free to leave an event after collecting five cards.

- Use a cell phone app to scan business cards immediately, and send an email to those individuals to make a connection.

Chapter 7
Step Two: Keep Track

"Energy and persistence conquer all things."

Benjamin Franklin (1706-1790),
author and original Founding Father of the USA

I HAVE USED a variety of recordkeeping systems for tracking who I follow up with over the 15 years I have been networking for business. I have found the important thing is not which system you use, but that you *pick one and stick to it.*

You need to track two things: the appointments in your calendar, and the number of times and methods you use to follow up with your A and B contacts.

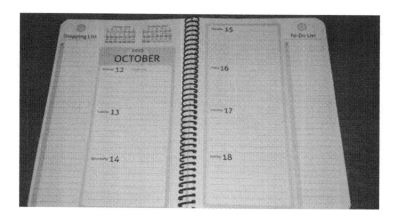

Calendar

Before trying any system, analyze your habits and see what types of tools you are currently using. For example, is your iPhone or

Android smartphone an appendage you use from the time it wakes you up in the morning until you check your email or texts the last thing before going to sleep at night? If so, you may prefer to put everything into your mobile phone.

Or are you old school, and like to be able to glance at a paper calendar you carry around with you? Or do you like to carry a yellow notepad, and write down everything there?

In my first network marketing business, my early business partner and mentor used a simple yellow pad and a paper calendar to track what she was doing. I tried doing that, and found it didn't work as well for me. Although I would cross off the names of people I had called or contacted, this system didn't easily allow for tracking multiple "touches." I would have to periodically go through the used sheets to make sure I didn't miss anyone's name to contact again. My calendar was a separate book from the yellow pad, and for me it was cumbersome.

If you are using a paper calendar, can you carry it with you everywhere? At a recent networking meeting, I wanted to make an appointment with a massage therapist. She had left her appointment book in the car. I was perplexed, as this was a business meeting she attends every week. I didn't understand why she doesn't routinely carry her appointment book. I had to rush off to another meeting and couldn't wait for her to go to the car to get it, so we put off making the appointment. I left it up to her to get back to me, but she did not. You don't want potential customers or clients like me to have to wait when they WANT to make an appointment. So if you use a paper calendar, make sure you always carry it with you.

If you use a calendar system on your mobile phone, does it synchronize with your other devices? To keep from overbooking yourself, you don't want to enter the information about appointments more than once. I use Google Calendar on all my devices, and they synchronize wirelessly, so I don't have to worry about doing it manually. The Google Calendar also synchronizes with Outlook on my computer. And if any of your events are on *Meetup.com*, you can also add them to your Google Calendar, so everything takes care of itself. Because I am using this calendar, I have moved away from using a paper calendar.

More and more I find my mobile devices are the ones I use preferentially, as they liberate me from having to be in front of the computer.

Tracking Follow-up Touches

Another mentor of mine, Todd Falcone, uses a book with lines for names, and boxes to check off. He purchases the book, so he doesn't have to make the record sheet himself. Todd is a master at *the cold call*, and *follow-up calls*. He uses this book to track when he calls contacts.

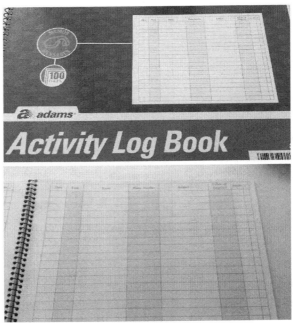

At a workshop on follow-up, a couple participants mentioned their methods:

- Attach individual business cards to a sheet in a notebook. You then use dividers to place them in alphabetical order.

- Photocopy each business card to a sheet, and place it in a notebook

- Remind yourself who you need to contact by having a section in the front of a notebook with the months or days of the week. Put individual sheets there, and make notes on them as you contact each person.

In Mark and Rene Yarnell's book, *Your First Year In Network Marketing,* they suggested writing the name of a prospect at the top of an index card, and their phone number next to it.

I had tried using sheets in a notebook, as mentioned above, but I didn't need a whole piece of paper until I sat with the prospect, or had a long conversation with them. And I needed a way to keep track of the number of times and ways I contacted each person I met before I was able to interview them.

So before I went digital, I used a modified version of tracking on index cards. In doing so, I found it easier to staple business cards onto a 3x5 card and keep them in a file. I made notes on the cards about the content of conversations I had with the person, and the date when I contacted them.

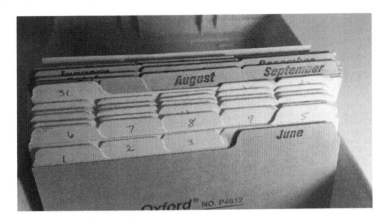

Just like what I had seen in the dentist's office, I set up a separate small file box so after I had spoken to a contact and had arranged for an appointment to call back or meet them for coffee, I moved the card to that location in the file. I had tabs for the month, and then tabs for the days. I moved the tabs for the days to the successive month as the calendar progressed. The card file was small enough that I could carry it with me in the car, and make calls on the go.

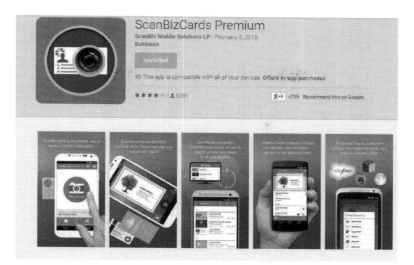

Now I use the ScanBizCards app on my smartphone or the BizRunner app. They allow me to scan a business card, and send an email within 24 to 48 hours. I can make notes about them at the time I scan their business card. I usually sit in my car after an event and do it, so they get an email from me before they even get to their office. When I can do that, I get a much quicker response to my emails.

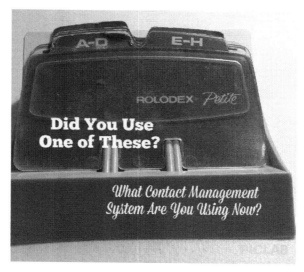

Digital Contact Manager

Depending on your budget, there are some high tech systems that will let you track your contacts. They do this with a variety of tools, and depending on how elaborate they are, they can integrate emails, documents, jobs, faxes, and scheduling for individual accounts. This is called a **Customer Relationship Management (CRM)** system. Whatever CRM system you use, be sure to collect and record personal information about people.

> **Building Your Contact Manager**
> 1. Birthday and Birthplace
> 2. Family Details
> 3. Education
> 4. Connections/Groups They Belong To
> 5. Accomplishments
> 6. Fun Activities
> 7. Desired Referrals

I use a Contact Manager in my online greeting card company that allows me to make notes about my contacts, as well as keep track of the content of every card I have sent them. You can enter individual contacts one at a time, or upload contacts from other systems, like Outlook. You can also access the Contact Manager and send cards from a smartphone.

Some people get very proficient with Outlook, or with other digital systems like Google. No matter what system you are using, you need to be able to record personal information and access it when you need to.

You could also create an Excel spreadsheet that would allow you to track every time you contact the person, and how you do it. Then you would have the option of recording in the spreadsheet on your computer, or printing the spreadsheet out and writing on it.

Tips for Success:
1. Track appointments.
2. Track follow-up methods used.
3. Always have your appointment calendar with you.

Action Steps I Will Take Now:
- Pick a tracking system for contacts.
- Build in a reminder system.
- Be consistent in using the system to monitor how many times I follow up, and how.

Chapter 8
Step Three: Speak Their Language

"Your ability to communicate is an important tool in your pursuit of your goals, whether it is with your family, your co-workers or your clients and customers."

Les Brown,
motivational speaker and author

Seth Godin, well-known vice president of Yahoo and a marketing expert, coined the phrase "Permission Marketing" to describe marketing directed at those people who have given you permission to communicate with them. To me, it describes the relationship you have with anyone who has given you a business card or contact information. They have said YES to follow-up.

In the long run, it is more cost-effective to put people into your Contact Manager and stay in touch with them, than it is to keep going to meetings, collecting business cards, and never staying in touch with the contacts you make. But how will you do it?

In my working with clients, I have noticed most people have their favorite methods of follow-up. One client used the phone as his preferred method. He also sent emails to prospects, and scoffed at using other types of follow-up. He was very frustrated with the fact that few people took his calls or returned them. My advice to him was to ask his prospects how they preferred to be contacted, and then use that method as his first choice.

Follow-up Methods
1. In-Person Appointment
2. Email
3. Phone Calls
4. Texting/Instant Messenger
5. Social Media
6. Skype or FaceTime
7. Cards and Letters

If after my initial contact at a networking event, I have a scheduled *in-person* meeting with someone, I prepare for it by doing a little online investigation by searching on Google, or looking at their profile on LinkedIn or Facebook. If you choose to do this, it could give you information on any awards they've won or hobbies they may have. This isn't stalking; this is research and can be used in your meeting to break the ice.

At the time of the meeting, I use a form to collect their personal information (Appendix). I make lots of notes and ask questions about them, their families, their interests, and how they prefer to be contacted. In addition, I pay attention to the methods they use when they contact me. If possible, I try to follow suit.

Here is a graphic that shows the way I follow up with a possible customer to be able to set up an appointment to explain my product.

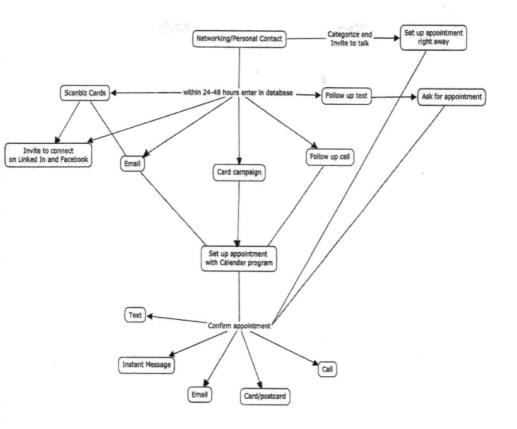

Method 1: In-Person Appointment

When you first meet someone, and you'd like to know more about that person, schedule an appointment right then to meet with them one-on-one. If you can, it might be convenient to meet immediately after the event. Always take your marketing materials with you, and have your calendar so you are prepared for a spontaneous meeting. Usually, however, you will schedule a later follow-up meeting to occur as soon as possible.

Use your follow-up appointment to get to know the person better, and to get a feeling for their level of interest in what you do. If they are interested in a sales presentation, by all means deliver one. But most of the time, they would rather enjoy getting to know you. This is an opportunity for you to decide how to proceed, and whether their interest is primarily to sell you their product or service.

A local representative of a weight loss program is notorious for saying he wants to meet with people because he is interested in their product or service. At the time of the meeting, he then suggests that if they give him referrals that lead to a sale, he might be able to use what they offer. To most people, this approach feels manipulative.

Realistically, there may be more than one person you meet who is selling the same product or service. You can't buy from all of them. And you may have a product they can use. Do your best to dissociate from the idea that you have to buy in order to get the sale. Would you ever think that way in a retail store?

The best way to approach people you don't know well is to use the first meeting as a "getting to know you" session. If they love what you are selling, great. But don't go into the meeting expecting to make a sale. It may take more than one in-person meeting to accomplish that. Just know you are a master of follow- up, and if they are a good candidate for your product or service, your persistence will pay off. Your goal is to teach them what a good referral is for you, and if appropriate, ask for referrals when you are together.

Method 2: Email

I've mentioned that I use the *ScanBizCards* app or the *BizRunner* app on my smartphone to first scan business cards I get, and then to send an email as soon as possible after I meet someone. In the past, the SanBizCards app lets me create an email I could use over and over, along with a way to make notes about the contact. It is more challenging to use now, so I have switched to the BizRunner app primarily.

I use Google Mail to keep in touch with contacts. I have also added a series of plugins to make emails more manageable. I have added *YesWare* to the mix, which lets me to track who opens the emails and choose to use another method to follow up with those who don't open them. In addition, it allows me to use templates for follow-up emails. I can track which ones get opened, and which don't, and decide how to modify them.

You can also use a system like *Constant Contact, Mail Chimp* or *AWeber*. Put your contacts into the database and send regular emails or bulletins (newsletters) to them. You may want to ask permission before putting contacts into an autoresponder program like Constant Contact, or use a double opt in method to make sure you get permission to continue sending group emails or newsletters.

Remember that most business people get hundreds of emails each day. Email has the advantage of being free, and if you appropriately personalize your emails, it may serve the purpose of keeping you front of mind for your prospects, clients, and customers.

I have gotten more responses to the emails I send immediately through ScanBizCards than when I wait. While I found no research using this follow-up method specifically, I was able to find research related to the effectiveness of quick follow-up to online leads. If you have a website, and are generating leads from it, it is essential you have a way to respond as fast as possible.

A research study of 42 companies published in the *Harvard Business Review* indicates that when potential customers are contacted within an hour, companies are nearly seven times as likely to have meaningful conversations that could result in a sale. In other words, the faster you follow up, the more likely it is you will make a sale.

Unfortunately, most companies do not follow up in a timely fashion. In an audit of 2,241 U.S. companies, only 37% of companies responded to an online lead within an hour, 16% responded within the first 24 hours, 24% took more than 24 hours, and 23% never responded.

Method 3: Phone Calls

The phone is one of the easiest tools for follow-up, and one commonly used. Unfortunately, many people do not answer their phones for a variety of reasons. They can be busy and not able to answer. One of my business associates noted, it annoys her when a sales person she has met doesn't ask or send an email before calling her to push the latest product or sale. When you call and leave a message, they may not call you back. Messages can get lost, or erased, so don't take it personally if you don't get a return call.

If you use the phone as a major method of follow-up, be sure to combine it with other methods. In the past 15 years, I have met very few people who prefer to be called, and do not have an email on their business card. It is rare, but it does happen. Again, adjust your follow-up method to suit the person you are connecting with.

When contacts who do not return calls, consider scheduling a phone appointment. Then you show you are considerate of their time, and you can tell them what you want to discuss with them, so they can be prepared.

Method 4: Texting/Instant Messenger

Many people prefer to use texting or Instant Messenger. They are much faster to respond to a text or Facebook message than to a call. Of course, you need a mobile phone to be able to send text messages.

Be sure to ask your contact the best way to communicate with them. One of my business associates said she prefers texting, or instant message, because then it is up to her to respond. She only uses the phone rarely, and it irritates her to get calls during her work day by sales reps hawking their skin creams.

Method 5: Social Media

Social media is a moving target, and it includes whatever is trending at the moment. At first it was MySpace; then Facebook, LinkedIn, and Twitter; and now YouTube, Instagram, Pinterest, Google+, and more. The trick is to use the ones your target market uses.

Choose to follow or "friend" your customers or clients. See what they post about. What is going on in their business and their lives? This is part of getting to know them. Can you respond to a request? Comment as a friend would about what they write about:

- A recent conference they attended

- An upcoming vacation

- Illness in a family member, parent or friend

- A new baby

- Their birthday

If you are a small business owner, you have limited time for each and every aspect of your business, so you may also want to estimate what being active on social media costs you in terms of time spent. There are tools available to consolidate your time, so that when you post on Facebook or LinkedIn, for example, you are also posting to your Twitter account. Look into these, or find an assistant or virtual assistant who will keep up with all of it for you.

Another thing to consider is who you want to reach. Do you have a clear picture of who your ideal customer is? It will vary depending on your business and audience.

Are they local or international? Men or women? Baby Boomers, GenX, GenY or another generation? You may find they prefer to communicate via Facebook Messenger rather than the phone or email. You must tailor your social media approach to best connect with your prospects.

With over 1 billion people now on Facebook, and over 400 million users on LinkedIn, can you afford to turn up your nose, or throw up your hands? It can be an asset to your business. This is especially true if you can link your networking on social media to your in-person networking: find people at events and connect with them online, or fi nd them online and see them at events.

As in all things, content is king. Pay attention to what other people post that you like to read. The Social Media Examiner advises varying your posts. Alternate your status updates with images and videos. And generally speaking, it doesn't matter which platform we are talking about. You get more attention when you alternate the types of posts you make.

Since the goal is to attract followers, you do want to avoid the obvious polarizing posts on sex, politics, religion, and sports. Limit the posts about your business, except perhaps on your business page. And please, unless you just can't stand it, no ranting. There will be people who agree with you, but your goal is to attract people who may want to do business with you, not just use the platform because everyone is entitled to your opinion. You will turn more people off than you attract.

Method 6: Skype/FaceTime/Google Hangouts/Google Duo/Facebook Instant Messenger

I recently met a professional who was looking for referrals to couples in trouble. She is a couples' therapist, and is using Skype to meet with people virtually. You can do this as well. It can add a personal touch to an interaction, more personal in many ways than a phone call. But be aware that your web camera sees things in back of you as well as your face. I have purchased a Japanese screen that I put up in back of my chair to hide the distractions of my bookcase, plants, animals walking around, etc.

Perfecting your office lighting might also be something you can look into. According to Remy Haynes, professional photographer, "From the front, side is best. Direct overhead light isn't flattering to anyone. These slight changes can make a nice, professional difference in how you appear on camera."

I have used Skype to talk to a possible virtual assistant. Although she is local, having to drive to a meeting takes a minimum of an hour round trip. With Skype, we were able to stay in our offices and have an hour-long discussion without wasting the time in the car. It isn't for everyone, but it might be a good alternative for people you have met with in person and want to follow up with.

Another new option, is Google Duo. It is platform similar to Skype that allows you to have video calling. Joel Comm, who I follow for his take on video and other innovations, is watching a variety of live video tools. Keep your eye onvideo.

One of my business associates lives in Scotland, while I live in California. I was on my way to the pet supply store for some exotic cat food and heard the phone ringing in a strange way. It was my associate "calling" me on Facebook Instant Messenger. Just recently, Facebook has added Facebook Live as well as video instant messaging. Bottom line, video in addition to texting, tokeep in touch more personally and economically.

Method 7: Cards and Letters

After reading Bob Burg's *Endless Referrals*, I started sending cards to everyone I met at events. Mary Kay Ash, the developer of the Mary Kay skincare line, advocated sending three cards a day. As I was researching this topic, I found that virtually every expert on networking advocates keeping in touch with prospects by using cards and letters.

Harvey McKay, author of *Dig Your Well Before You're Thirsty*, would find out about the person he connected with, and the types of things they were interested in. Then if he spotted an article on a topic they might find interesting, he sent it to them with a note.

I did this recently after I learned a person in my network selling reverse mortgages is passionate about gardening. But not just any gardening. She is an expert on California native plants that are at home in the Chaparral ecosystem where we live. Since we have an ongoing drought, I thought she might want to connect with companies she could partner with. She has the vision to help people who are eligible for reverse mortgages to get the money they need to convert their grass into a carpet of native plants. I sent her clippings about landscape and construction companies that might be potential partners.

When was the last time you shared something of value with a prospect? Google might be helpful here as well. When you read any magazine, newsletter, or other source of information, think about how you can share the information with your prospects, customers, and clients. What might bring value to their day?

Cards show people how important they are to you. It is a very effective follow-up technique that few people do. When you start sending cards, you stand out from the crowd. And it can be effective as well. According to the Direct Marketing Association, the response rate for direct mailing is 3.4 percent. This refers to the type of blanket mailings we all get at home. Imagine how much more effective mail from someone you know can be. And the more personalized the mail, the more likely the person will keep it for future reference.

"Thanks Kaaren Douglas for the card. It brought a smile to my face." A friend from the Chamber had a fire at her home that displaced her and her husband, and burned many of the paintings she had finished. She liked the card so much that she posted it on Facebook with this thank you.

I use an *online greeting card system* now because it allows me to automate the cards I send. These are real cards that you create with the ease of email, and then the company prints them for you, and mails them. Their quality is high; I just spoke to a friend I have been sending cards to for years, and she didn't realize I wasn't writing them out myself.

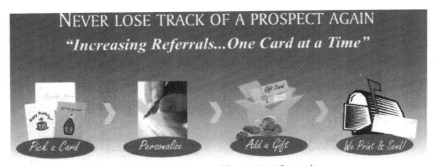

- Extensive Card Catalog with both Business and Personal greeting cards
- Custom Cards, write in your own Personal Handwriting Fonts, Add Pictures, and Edit Pictures with Picture Plus
- Insert Gifts: Gift Cards, Sweets & Treats, Seasonal Gifts, Books and Magazines
- Online calendar and reminder system to manage contact information and special occasions
- Online Contact Manager to help you organize and add contact information

www.kaarendouglas.biz

As a time-saver, you can create a card once and send it over and over again. You can program the system to send out birthday cards, holiday cards, marketing cards, whatever type you want to send. I send about 100 cards each month. I would never be able to hand write that many with the ease I have with this online card system. And now I have a record of everyone I have written to, and a copy of every card I have sent. In the past, I might buy cards and forget to send them. Or write a note and forget what I said. That doesn't happen now.

Whenever I meet with someone, with the company's new app on my phone, I can take a "selfie" of the two of us at the time of the meeting, put them into my Contact Manager, and send them a card right from my phone. The system helps me remember to send them a birthday card, anniversary card, and even cards to their kids, if appropriate.

As T. Harv Eker, author of *Secrets of the Millionaire Mind* said, sending a card impacts your contacts in multiple ways. It conveys a message. It conveys emotion. It is an object that can be saved and viewed later. Unlike email, which only has a left-brain impact, a greeting card has a right-brain impact as well. And if you really want to make sure the card is not discarded, do as I do, and take a picture of you the person you have been talking to at the end of a meeting, and send it back to them in a card thanking them for their time. It is the rare person who will throw away their own picture. The cards have your contact information on the back, so even if the recipient loses your business card, they will have your greeting card.

Tips for Success:
1. Ask people you meet the best way to contact them.
2. Take action within 24-48 hours after meeting.
3. Use at least 3 methods of follow-up so you know you will be getting through to them.

Action Steps I Will Take Now:

• Scan or enter contact information within 24-48 hours after meeting someone into my CRM system of choice.

• Respond to any website inquiries within 24- 48 hours.

• Use consistent methods of follow-up (pick three):

• Set an appointment as soon as I meet someone

• Phone call

- Email

- Instant Messenger

- Facebook connect

- LinkedIn connect

- Follow-up card or letter

- Skype or FaceTime

- Other

Chapter 9
Step Four: Say It Right

"Think twice before you speak, because your words and influence will plant the seed of either success or failure in the mind of another."

Napoleon Hill (1883-1970),
author

IF I SAY, "Create scripts…" do you see a playwright slaving on her computer to come up with just the right words for her characters? Or do you get a knot in your stomach remembering the last telemarketerwho interrupted your dinner to read you their pitch?

Hopefully, you can try a mental chiropractic to adjust your discomfort and reconcile the negatives to consider another interpretation. According to sales and scripting coach Eric Lofholm, scripts are merely words in sequence that have meaning. We all use scripts daily. We do it unconsciously, and to our advantage. For example, when you attend an event, you use a script to describe what you do, and what you are looking for.

The advantages of purposely creating a script are:

- You know what you will say.

- You have less anxiety talking to people you don't know, or speaking in front of a crowd.

- You can judge the effectiveness of what you said.

- You can choose to change what you say the next time if it didn't have the desired effect.

An email template is another form of a "script," as is anything that communicates the same information over and over for multiple people, like a form letter.

I have created scripts for networking events and follow-up emails. I have scripts for follow-up calls and calls to people I haven't spoken to for a while. I have created scripts for my assistant to use when calling my customers. The greeting cards I send to prospects after I meet with them use a form of script, as I create the card once, and send the same card in follow-up every time.

Once when I was talking to a network marketer about the concept of scripts, she said, "I don't believe in scripts." And yet I had heard her many times on the phone with prospects, and she was successful because she communicated the same information every time.

Leaders in the network marketing business promote the script concept, because they know it will keep their new business partners out of trouble. The challenge is knowing what to say, and not saying too much.

To use verbal scripts effectively, write them down. Then practice them over and over, until the information comes out naturally. Sometimes it might be a good idea to find a friend with whom you can practice scripts. Try calling each other, and run through your script as if you're making a cold call. Your friend can advise you on what sounds good and what sounds like you are reading.

First decide the different types of scripts you will need.

Types of Scripts
1. Networking
2. Emails
3. Telephone
4. Social Media
5. Cards and Letters

Script 1: Networking

If you have ever been to a networking event, you have heard good and bad commercials. In this context, commercials are the short little speeches people give in the front of the room, or in front of the group, that attempt to excite, interest, and motivate their listeners to say, "Tell me more."

What characterizes the poor ones? You know, before even being asked. The person hems and haws, or uses "seller language," or tells you about their great business opportunity, ignoring the fact that everyone in the room already has a business or they wouldn't be there. They may also go on and on in front of the room, exceeding the time allotted.

What does a good commercial sound like? You remember it. Maybe it made you laugh. Perhaps it was dramatic, or the person did a "show and tell" that captured your attention. Think about what you liked and didn't like about the commercials you have heard. How can you make yours better?

In one of the networking groups I attend, a business member has a store where she sells lingerie, and sex toys. When she gets up to give her self-introduction, she usually shows everyone the personal vibrator she suspends as a necklace around her neck. Yes, she gets everyone's attention.

Casey Eberhart, the Ideal Networker, uses a different approach. He advocates finding the contacts you want to talk to, getting to know something about *them,* and then talking about them when it is time to do your own commercial. In other words, you do a mini-testimonial for them.

For most of us, it is natural to be uncomfortable in front of an audience; even standing in front of a small group can make your hands sweat and your heart race. To feel more comfortable, plan out what you want to say; write it down; and practice, practice, practice. Answer the question, "What can you do for me?" Use a prop, make a joke at your own expense and let people know exactly what type of referral you are looking for. And when a script works, keep using it.

Amy Cuddy, social psychologist, has done research demonstrating that striking "power poses" can improve your confidence level. These poses raise the testosterone level, and reduce the stress hormone cortisol. To feel more comfortable getting up in front of the group, take some private time, and practice standing like Wonder Woman, arms on hips. During the presentation, lifting up your arms in a V shape, like a runner at the end of the race, is another power pose you can try.

One of the networking groups in our area has attracted a woman with a unique approach to exercise. She teaches *hoop classes.* So what does she bring up with her when she does her commercial? A hula hoop. I saw her do a presentation while using the hoola hoop the entire time. I don't know how she did it. I was in awe, and I won't forget it or her. During her presentation, she moved with the hoop in a way that made sure she used "power poses" throughout.

How will you know a script is working? Listen for laughter. Watch to see if people are paying attention. And when people come up to you later to ask questions, you know you have a hit on your hands.

If you need even more help, think about joining *Toastmasters.* This worldwide network of groups meets to practice public speaking. You might even learn to enjoy it.

Before I attend a networking event, I write out a script for my 30-second "pitch." I have attended workshops and written hundreds of scripts to hone my skills. When I was in a networking group that met every week, I changed the script weekly to teach about a different aspect of my business. The one constant was my tagline: "Trust Me, I'm a Doctor. The Follow Up Doctor."

When you plan to attend a networking event, prepare to give a pitch to the room, as well as what you will say to people one-on-one. Here is an example of one of my front-of-theroom commercials:

> *Dr. Kaaren Douglas, The Follow Up Doctor. When you come to events like this one, do you collect any of these? [I hold up a stack of business cards.]*
>
> *What do you do with them? Do you take them home and toss them on your desk? [Put them down on the table, or stuff into my coat pocket.]*
>
> *Do you feel overwhelmed when you look at them lying there? Do you have one of these? [I hold up my smartphone.]*
>
> *Let me show you how to use it to convert those cards into contacts you can follow up with before you get back to the office. Let me help you eliminate overwhelm. Dr. Kaaren Douglas. Trust Me, I'm a Doctor. The Follow Up Doctor.*

As you are meeting new people at the event, what do you tell them about yourself and your product or service? When I joined *Worthwhile Referral Services*, a Southern California networking group, many years ago, we were taught to describe our business briefly, and then ask the other person what type of referrals they were looking for. As you work on a quick description of your business, stay away from titles, like "I sell insurance," and instead tell the person how you benefit your clients. "I help people protect their assets." What you want is for the other person to ask, "Really? How do you do that?"

For example, Joel W. is a Realtor, and if he just said he sold real estate, how would he be differentiating himself from the other Realtors in the room? When he identified a niche market he likes to work with, he wore a cowboy hat, and said, "I'm a horse owner myself, so I really enjoy helping others who would like to purchase equestrian properties." Let your commercial tell the listener how you are special. And then cue it in to the types of referrals you are looking for. The goal at any event is to identify people who you want to meet again. Leave them wanting more, so you can continue to talk at another time.

As you sort through the new people you are meeting, and have decided someone is an "A" contact, have a script you can use right then to set up a time to meet later. For example, when I was an ambassador for the Chamber of Commerce, I used this type of script:

> *Hi, I'm Dr. Kaaren Douglas, The Follow Up Doctor. I help business owners develop a system of follow-up that works for them. What is it that you do?*
>
> *That's interesting. What do you like best about it?*
>
> *What types of referrals are you looking for?*
>
> *Is there anyone here you'd like to meet? [If I can introduce them to someone at the event, I take them over to the person and do the introductions, and then move on. If not...]*

I'd like to learn more about you and your business, to learn how we can help each other. Let's set a time for us to meet. Is next Tuesday at 2pm or Wednesday at 4pm better for you?

[If they are not able to check their appointment calendar at that time follow with...] Great. I'll send you an email with a couple of dates and times that work for me. Is that an OK place to start? Let me confirm I have your email address.

Script 2: Email

One thing I like when using *ScanBizCards* is that I can scan a business card, and send a stock email and an invitation to become part of my LinkedIn network from my smartphone immediately after meeting a person at an event. As I mentioned before, I have been known to sit in my car, where I have a travel desk, and send my first emails within an hour after I have met the person. While emails have become less and less effective, since people get barraged with them every day, these "Johnny-on-the-spot" emails are more likely to get a response.

Decide on a few types of emails that you send on a regular basis, and create templates you can use over and over. You can integrate them into your AWeber, Mail Chimp or Constant Contact account to build your list. YesWare allows you to create custom templates within Gmail that save time.

Can you give someone a referral? An email introduction is the way to go. The Introduction should include both persons' names, a brief description of what they do, why you think the referral would be good for both parties, and their email addresses and phone numbers. All of these are essential elements so the people involved can contact each other, and you step out of the mix.

Recently I met a cycling/exercise coach on a plane, and referred her to a friend who is the sales manager for a cycling store. Their introduction to each other looked like this:

Subject: Introductions
Hi [Name of Contact],
Just want to introduce you to my friend [Name of Person you are referring], who is the Sales Manager at [Name of Business]. He has extensive experience in the cycle world, as I told you. He has worked at a number of bike stores, and worked in banking and specialized marketing systems before that. He can fill you in. His cell is _____. He is looking forward to

connecting with you and learning more about what you do so he can pass it on to appropriate customers at the store.

[Name of Other Contact],

I want to introduce you to [Name of Person being referred], the cycle/exercise coach I met on the plane back from Denver. She can tell you more about her business. She currently works with clients in _____ area, as well as long distance clients, including some in our area. Her website is _____. There is a great picture of her on the site. I loved her enthusiasm, and believe she would be a great contact for you. Her phone is _____.

Do you have a newsletter you send out regularly? Or a blog you link to your Facebook page or Instagram? Do you have a free gift you can give if a person agrees to be on your email list?

Before you sign someone up without their permission, send an email to your contact and ask if you can put them on your email list. Not everyone will agree, but that's okay. For every no there is someone else who will say yes, and you don't want to annoy people who are reluctant to say no to your face. Many of the systems have a double opt-in procedure, so when a person gets your email they have to click on the email to agree to receive more from you and be put on your list. This assures you that they indeed want to stay in contact.

This process suggests the need for templates you can use over and over. Try writing one version, see what kind of response you get, and then modify it slightly and try a different version and see if you get a better response. You can also collect emails from other marketers and place them in a "swipe" file. (A swipe file is one in which you copy and paste emails or sales copy other people have used.)

See what kinds of headings and text appeal to you, and try using a version of it to send to your contacts. There is a reason effective marketers use the same types of emails, with certain titles and content. They work. Just copy what is working for others, and modify it for yourself.

Be cautious about using certain terms that may push your email into the spam folder of your recipient. In your subject line, avoid terms like "offer," "as seen," "double your," "for only," and "FREE." Within the body of the text, your email could look like spam if it has more than one line of words in all caps, or claims not to be spam. A few other words that might keep your messages from getting to your recipients are "success," "wealth," "money," "fortune," "incredible," and similar boasting.

The goal of your emails as part of your overall follow-up system is to schedule a personal meeting with a prospect to get to know them. Then your emails will be part of your follow-up touches to keep them in the loop before and after they buy from you.

The best way to prevent problems with customers is to make sure you continue to keep in touch after they have bought from you. Keep in mind that they are also the ones who are more likely to buy from you again when you have a new product to offer. The more you keep in touch, the more likely they will respond.

You can also use email to ask for testimonials after someone has become your customer, or is using your service. Make it easy for them by supplying them with a format to help them create a memorable testimonial.

Great Testimonials Contain:
1. Name, Occupation, Location
2. Personal Story
3. Ways Product/Service is Used
4. How Product/Service has Been Helpful
5. Examples

Script 3: Telephone

When you are calling people, recognize they may not be able to talk at the time you reach them. If you reach their voice mail, be prepared with an appropriate script.

Here are a few examples of telephone scripts I have used:
Hi, is this [name of prospect]? This is Dr. Kaaren Douglas. It was great meeting you at [name of networking event or location where you met]. Is this a good time to talk? [If yes, proceed. If no, ask when it would be good to call back about setting up a time to get together.] *I'd like to learn more about you and your business so we can help each other. Let's set a time within the next couple of weeks when we can get together. Is next Tuesday at 2pm or Wednesday at 4pm better for you?* [Not able to check appointment book at that time.] *Great. I will send you an email with a couple of dates and times that work for me. Is that an OK place to start? Let me confirm I have your email address.*

If you get their voice mail, it could go like this:
Hi, this is Dr. Kaaren Douglas. It was great meeting you at [the networking event or location where you met]. *I'm calling to learn more about you and your business, and find out more about how we can help each other. I'd really like to talk to you. Please give me a call at* [tell them your phone number]. *I look forward to hearing from you. Again, my number is* [repeat your phone number].

Once someone has signed up as a customer, make sure you give them a follow-up call to make sure they are using the product, and to answer any of their questions. If there is a common problem among customers, you can ask about that. If they have ordered product, make sure you call after the time when they would have received it and started using it to make sure they are happy. If you are rendering a service, put a call in after the job to check in on their level of satisfaction.

If there is a problem, you can use another script to acknowledge it, or even prevent it. Keep in touch before problems occur. You can also ask your customers how to do a better job. Tell them about challenges you face, and ask how you can do better for them.

If someone is happy using your service or understands how it could be helpful to someone else, and you have spent time creating a relationship with them, ask for referrals. Go to their website and learn about their business. Give them referrals when you can, and any free products you have available. When you ask, you need to be specific about the types of referrals that will be most helpful to you. For example, what types of people do they know that you would like to meet for your business? The more specific you can be, the better, as most people appreciate the help in giving referrals.

Script 4: Social Media

As I have already mentioned, whenever I get a business card, or make a connection with a new person, I also invite them to connect with me on LinkedIn. In addition, I will reach out to them on Facebook, Google+, Twitter and any other social media I feel is appropriate for our connection.

Some people do not understand the merit of connecting on so-cial media platforms, but I see it as a way to be transparent to my friends and business contacts, and learn more about what is important to them as well. If you are connected to me, you will learn I value healthy eating, love my dogs and cats, and enjoy travel. As much as possible, I avoid controversial postings.

My goal with social media is to keep in touch with my contacts. If possible, I also want to connect with people I esteem: business people like Bob Burg or Joel Comm, or fiction writers like Mara Purl and Nat Russo. With Bob Burg, although we have never met in person, we have become friends on Facebook who communicate directly, because we share an interest in animal rescue. I met Joel Comm at the AuthorU May Extravaganza, a yearly writers' meeting. We keep in touch through Facebook. Mara Purl is a friend from a book group I attended more than 10 years ago, and we have kept in touch through email, phone, and postings on Facebook as well. Nat Russo is an author I found on Twitter, whose blog I follow because of his writing tips. We are also connected on Facebook, and I pass on his postings to my contacts on a regular basis.

When you send someone a friend request, or a request to connect with you on a platform, personalize it whenever possible. For example, let them know why you want to connect with them. Do you value their postings? Let them know why and how they have enriched your life. At the same time, you can use a template for the request,including your business contact information.

How about doing a testimonial for someone on Facebook or LinkedIn, or even a video testimonial on YouTube? If you want to build a following, and stay connected with others, focus on what you can do for them. Use the sametestimonial outline when you give someone else a testimonial,either through email, social media or video.

You can create a group and invite your connections to join, either on Facebook or LinkedIn. You can create an event, or announce an event, and let people in your network know about it. One of the networkers in my area routinely schedules events on Facebook and Meetup as a way of encouraging the most people to attend. I have created scripts (standard replies) to send people to my Facebook business page. LinkedIn likes scripts (standard replies) so much it provides you with an appropriate one to send from their app to acknowledge business anniversaries, or birthdays. I have found my contacts appreciate these little messages. I have been using them for just a couple of months, and have scheduled two meetings with local people I want to connect with.

Script 5: Cards and Letters

Form letters and card campaigns in a system lend themselves to be used again and again to save time. In my online greeting card system, the mail merge program is called a Campaign. The goal is to take the time to create a personal card, and send it over and over to different people or to a large group all at once.

This is how I create my holiday cards. It is possible to create individual cards as well, and use them judiciously during the year to keep in touch with someone.

It is important to send personal cards and letters after meeting with someone. If you choose to use handwritten cards instead, be sure to have stationery and stamps on hand so you can send a card or note immediately after meeting with someone. You can write out a template, and use it over and over. I also clip and send articles of interest when possible.

In addition, you can send announcements of a new product, an upcoming sale, new services you are offering, and notification of new staff you are working with. Send thank you cards after meetings, for referrals and for being a customer. Send reminder cards for yearly service or for a yearly anniversary.

Does sending cards work? According to the Direct Marketing Association, the response rate for direct blanket mailing we all get at home is 3.4 percent. The more personalized the mail, the more likely the person will keep it for future reference.

Here are a few responses I received after I started sending cards to contacts:

Wow, thanks for the Starbucks card. Perfect choice! I assume the card you sent me was from your company. I like it. I'll be in touch. D.G., Insurance Agent

Kaaren, You are so sweet. Thanks for the card and treats for Duke [his dog]. That was very nice of you. What are you doing on Sunday? Want to meet for coffee or a glass of wine? Let me know. Also you should come with me to the huge LinkedIn event on Tuesday: over 200 people expected. C.K., President, CEO, CKME Group, Inc.

What a wonderful card. Love the presentation, love the pictures, really love the words. I am so happy that you love your Mini and that the entire crew valued your business and treated you so wonderfully. Thank you so much for your patronage and I hope the next time you're in, you come by and say hello. L. B, President, Auto Dealership

Tom Hopkins built a real estate business with sale of $10 million by sending out 10 thank you cards daily. Mary Kay Ash built a $1.2 billion business by advocating her sales reps send three personal "thank you's" every day. How will you choose to use this tool?

> **Good Scripts**
> 1. Generate a response.
> 2. Contain humor when appropriate.
> 3. Always contain your tagline.

Action Steps I Will Take Now:

- Write a 30-second commercial.

- Write a 60-second commercial.

- Create a text I can send on Facebook or LinkedIn to generate interest, and help set up appointments.

- Write an email I can use to follow up every time I meet someone new.

- Send a greeting card, note or article to someone I have met.

Chapter 10
Step Five: Follow Up Every Day

"Patience, persistence and perspiration make an unbeatable combination for success."

Napoleon Hill (1883-1970),
author

THE FIVE EASY STEPS I have described are most effective when they become habits. And that means you need to integrate some type of follow-up into every workday.

> **Habits help you be more efficient, because you:**
> • Don't have to plan as much.
> • Don't have to think as much.
> • Will get things done.
> • Are consistent.

How are you currently including follow-up in your schedule? I have found the more networking events I attend, the more time I need to devote to inputting contacts into my database, and making sure I reconnect with them.

I created a schematic diagram with the *CMap* program. With this program you can easily create a graphic for yourself that shows how you plan to follow up with contacts. If you are lucky enough to have an assistant, the CMap will show them what steps are in your plan. It will allow you to identify areas you can turn over to them.

My schematic for follow-up includes multiple touches for every viable contact over time, and I make sure I include blocks of time in my schedule every day to make calls and schedule appointments.

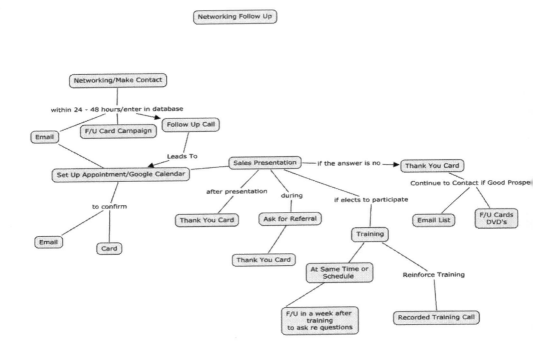

Multiple authors have defined their plans for follow-up. For example, in *Networking is a Contact Sport,* Joe Sweeney talks about his "5/10/15 Program." It consists of having five in-person meetings with new people per day. These can be any kind of contact with someone new, like at the coffee shop or the gas station. It all counts. Then he sends out 10 personal cards, letters or personal emails per day. Sweeney advocates sending heartfelt cards, newspaper clippings and books to people as follow-up. In addition, he makes 15 follow-up phone calls per day.

I am not sure how realistic Sweeney's plan is for most people. His suggestions make it obvious that without organization, no one could expect to accomplish what he suggests.

Andrea Nierenberg, in *Nonstop Networking*, describes her "2-2-2 Strategy." She attends two meetings of an organization; meets and exchanges business cards with two people at those meetings; and arranges two follow-up meetings for breakfast, lunch, or coffee. Since only 4% of mail is personal, she is another advocate of sending thank you notes, birthday cards, and clippings of interest to her contacts, because it has a positive impact. Her personal note plan includes sending three greeting cards each day in addition to thank you notes and follow-up notes. Then she sends three extra notes and three extra personal emails, and makes three extra phone calls per week to keep in touch with her network.

Her plan is perhaps more reasonable and achievable, but it too demands terrific organizational skills. Tracking is critical to make sure the best contacts you have are hearing from you regularly.

Sheldon and Hadley, in *The Smart Woman's Guide to Networking*, remarked that there are people who write notes and never send them, simply because they don't have stamps handy. If you are like me and hate going to the post office, or never have the right cards or stationery, you can solve this dilemma by using the *online greeting card system* I have previously described.

Seven Touches Within a Week
1. Send an email after a meeting.
2. Send a thank you card after a meeting.
3. Give a referral.
4. Request to connect on LinkedIn.
5. Invite to an event.
6. Connect on Facebook.
7. Follow up on an introduction.

Follow-up does not stop when the sale is made. Your current clients, customers and referral sources need to be remembered regularly. I suggest a plan to connect with them at least quarterly.

They need to hear from you about how you appreciate their business or assistance. When someone has been with you for some time, reach out to them during the year to let them know you are thinking of them. If someone sends you a referral, be sure to let them know how that went. Did it generate new business for you? How about sending them a thank you gift? I have found that brownies speak volumes!

Older Contacts and Follow-up

If it has been one to two years since you spoke to someone, look at your notes about that person and decide if they are a Category A, B, or C contact at this point. If you still want to keep in touch with them, send a card, an article, a cartoon, a media coverage announcement, or an update on what is going on with you. Then proceed to contact them every few months. Harvey Mackay recommends you freshen up each entry at least once every six months. If your contacts are older than two years, ask yourself if they will remember you. If not, let them go.

> **Tips for Follow-up**
> 1. Categorize your contacts.
> 2. Create a recordkeeping system.
> 3. Use a variety of followup methods.
> 4. Create scripts for follow-up.
> 5. Schedule follow-up every day.

Action Steps I Will Take Now:

- Schedule a block of time to make my follow-up calls and emails every day.

- Spend no more than 15 minutes twice a day on social media.

- Reduce my email inbox to 0 by the end of the week.

SECTION THREE

Chapter 11
Keep Your Customers

"You are never too old to set another goal or to dream a new dream."

C. S. Lewis (1898-1963),
novelist and Christian apologist

ONCE SOMEONE HAS BECOME A CUSTOMER OR CLIENT, it is essential to keep in contact with them. Retaining existing customers saves five to ten times what it costs to acquire new ones. And repeat customers tend to spend more money with you, up to 67% more than new customers.

Reasons Customers Leave

What will happen if you don't keep in touch with your customers? Won't they continue to be your customer or client if you provide a good product or service? Why would people stop doing business with you?

Poor follow-up is the biggest complaint customers have, according to the *Harvard Business Review*. Customers may leave because they believe you or your company are indifferent to them. After working so hard to acquire a customer base, you don't want it to disappear because of inattention.

Recently, one of my contacts on Facebook commented about how excited she was to get a "thank you" from a customer. Think about the last time someone expressed gratitude toward you. Did they thank you in person? Did you get an email? Did you get a thank you card? How did it make you feel?

Project that feeling onto your own customers and clients. I believe it is important to thank them. Most salespeople don't do that, or at least not often enough. What has been your experience as a customer? If your customers and clients hear "thank you" from you, it creates a stronger relationship with you. It is rare that I have ever received a thank you card from someone I have done business with. When it happens, that vendor really stands out.

See your customers in terms of their life-long value to your business, rather than just in terms of the immediate sale. When you do, it makes it easy to go the extra mile, and add more value to their purchase. Because it is an easy thing to do, I routinely add brownies to my thank you to a new customer. Another option is to remember your customers periodically by sending them a promotional item they can use. It makes your customers feel appreciated when they get one.

Some customer loss is inevitable. Each year you lose about 14% of your customers. Unless you continue to acquire customers, your customer numbers will decrease for a variety of reasons, some of which you cannot prevent. Of those that stop doing business with you:

- 1% die

- 3% move away

- 14% form relationships with other vendors that provide the same service or product

- 14% are unhappy

- 68% think you or your company are indifferent to their business

You might be able to prevent unhappy customers leaving by keeping an ongoing meaningful dialogue with them. And by the way, customers *do not* see your asking for additional orders, soliciting payment for services, scheduling appointments, or (shocking) sending a Christmas card as meaningful contact. Does this surprise you? When you contact them, let them know you appreciate them, and they will never fault you for ignoring them. But you need to do it on a regular basis.

Follow Up With Customers

Take what you have learned in the **Five Easy Steps** and apply it to keeping in touch with customers or clients.

Following up with customers is essential as part of the professional service you provide in appreciation of their working with you, or buying from you.

Master salesman Bob Golomb knows the value of follow-up. In every action, his focus was always to take care of the customer. This is how he did it: If a person bought a car from him, he was on the phone the next day to make sure they were happy. If a person did not buy from him, he still called the next day to thank them for stopping by.

Just as it is critical to keep a schedule of follow-up with potential customers, when people decide to buy from you, keep a regular schedule of follow-up with them.

Schedule

- Immediately after a customer buys from you, send them a personal email thanking them, and welcoming them as your customer.

- Same day as purchase, send a thank you card.

- Make sure you are connected on whatever platform they use on a regular basis. Thank them on that platform. If it is okay with them, post a picture with them on the platform. I always ask about photos, since some people would rather not have their picture on a public forum.

- Call or text new customers a week after they have become a customer, or after they have received their product or service from your company. Make sure they are happy. Ask if they have any questions. Ask if there is any other way you can help them, including referrals for their business.

- Follow up with an email that includes information they need, such as a customer service number they can call if they have concerns or questions.

- Send a follow-up card to arrive 30 days after the purchase, thanking them again, and making sure they are happy. If you can make them a limited- time offer, now is the time to do it. If you can reward a referral, make them an offer. Either way, ask for referrals.

- At 60 days, follow up again with a phone call or text to make sure they are using the product or service, and if they have questions, make sure they get answers.

- After the phone call, send an email. Do a customer survey, and offer an incentive to fill it out. Give them a coupon for a discount on future products or services that they can use or pass on.

- At 90 days, send another card, mentioning any other services or products they might be interested in. Ask for referrals.

- At 120 days, call again and ask for referrals.

Once the immediate "new customer" period is over, you can put them into your schedule for sending a newsletter; other autoresponders about your business, products, and services; and seasonal cards.

If you are using a service such as Mail Chimp or AWeber, create a specific autoresponder series for new customers. You can create emails that address the most commonly asked questions, and start the series when the person becomes a customer. The same is true with the *online greeting card company*. You can create a series of cards scheduled to be sent to new customers, at appropriate intervals, and they go out automatically. I choose to include a small thank you gift with the initial card I send to new customers.

Think long term with customers. Integrate your customer list into your prospect list to follow up through phone calls, email, newsletters, or links to your blog, and by sending cards and information they would appreciate. Follow up at least once per quarter. Since you are using a variety of methods, they won't feel like they are hearing from you too often. And they won't feel you are only contacting them to sell them something. If in doubt as to how often to follow up, ask the customer how often they would like to hear from you, and use that as a guideline.

Help your customers expand their business. Ask what they are looking for, and who they would like to be referred to within your database. Promote their business where possible on Facebook, Twitter or other platforms. Give testimonials for their business if possible. Write a review for them on Yelp.

You can also send your customers magazine articles from trade magazines or other resources. If you know what they are interested in, you can be on the lookout for information that will help them.

Always take responsibility for making contact with your customers. Remember, you want them to know you care about the relationship you have with them. If you contact them through a social media platform asking for a brief phone call, make sure you make it when they respond. Case in point, recently someone I have done business with in the past messaged me on Facebook and asked for my current cell phone number. He said he wanted to catch up. I responded within an hour, and gave him my number. I'm still waiting for the call.

When you call a customer, what will you say? Create specific scripts for these interactions, just as you create scripts (Chapter 9) for other purposes. And take notes. Ask how you can help them.

Are you selling nutritional products, or skincare, or some other consumable product that has special instructions? When you call the first time, advise your customer about anything they need to know. For example, new vitamins can sometimes cause stomach upset. In your first phone call, you can address this possibility in advance. Then you can give your customer some pointers about how to prevent it. This will prevent them from sending back the product before they have had a real trial. Or keep them from stopping it, and never telling you about it.

If you have a product that requires a little training to use, if you call and offer to help with the training before the customer has gotten frustrated, you may keep them from asking for a refund. You know what the pitfalls are of the product or service you are selling. Now is the time to make sure you address these, before they become a problem for your new customer.

Typical questions could include:

• Is there any way I can help?

• How can we improve the product or service?

• What would make you more satisfied?

Create an Action Plan

A good way to follow up, especially with customers, is to think about how you can help them. According to Michelle Lederman, you can live the Law of Giving by deciding to help your contacts and customers by deciding who you will help, what you will do, when you can do it, and choosing a different action plan for each person. For example, you could decide to connect two people in your network to each other, invite one of your customers or contacts to an event you have heard about, or send an article or link to someone who could benefit.

Bob Friedenthal, of the EdgeUp Networks, described a new system their company has just implemented that will make it easier to give and get referrals on LinkedIn. Social Sync allows you to readily evaluate if your connections give referrals to others. It also system allows you to send and track interactions and referrals within LinkedIn.

Your goal should be to make your customers raving fans. One way to do that is to keep connecting, and doing more for them. With my customers and people who give me referrals, as I noted before, I send brownies. For people who sign up as business partners, I send a book.

I am always looking for ways I can be of service, say thank you, be a connector, and create value for customers.

Chapter 12
Stay Connected

"What do I care? I barely knew the man. I saw him three times a year. Not enough to call him a friend. And every time I saw him, he was trying to sell me something. This is not friendship."

—Gabrielle Zevin,
The Storied Life of A.J. Fikry, 2014

AT THE BEGINNING of the book about A.J. Fikry's life, he is an unhappy man who has lost his wife, and whose only pleasure is to get drunk so he can "see" and talk to her again. He owns a bookstore, and is visited by a new representative of a publishing company he has been dealing with for years. He is complaining about his lack of relationship with the prior sales representative he saw three times a year, when he is told the man had died and this new rep is his replacement. As he says, you cannot build a friendship when either party is focused on selling, instead of on the other person. Friendship is the only thing that will sustain longterm relationships.

There are different types of friendships. Some people you meet at work, and don't see outside of the confines of the business. Others you meet at church, or while you are pursuing a hobby you love, like people who share your love of old cars, gardening, or skiing. With these friends, you are social, but not intimate. What you reveal to each other is fairly superficial, albeit cordial.

Acquaintances like these are important to building your network, as Gladwell discussed in *The Tipping Point*. For connectors, those who have the most acquaintances have the most power. If you are a connector with a large network, you can function as a trusted advisor to others, becoming someone others want to stay connected to because you know so many people, and are willing to share.

For acquaintances to move to deeper friendships takes time, effort and interest. It means you must lower your guard, and reveal more of your true self. And you can't skip ahead. I just had an encounter with someone who did not get this at all. I shared with her a family situation, because it seemed relevant for the discussion we were having, and she used it as a jumping off point to give me unsolicited advice. She may have thought she was helping, but the reaction I had was to shut down, and just wait for her to quit talking. Unfortunately, she does not understand that intimacy takes time to develop, and it cannot be rushed.

With some business contacts, you may never go beyond a friendly hello, and you never know much more about them except what their business is. If you are in doubt about what level friendship you have with someone, ask yourself if they would remember you if you didn't talk to them for an extended period of time. If not, would you like to have more of a relationship, and see it grow over time?

Friendships that last must be built on true concern and caring for the other person. That means taking time to learn about the other person, and finding out what is important to them. As Bob Burg and John David Mann say in their book, *Go-Givers Sell More,* think of your process as farming. The business connections that grow into something more depend on many factors. All you can control is what you invest in cultivating, watering and nurturing, so down the road you can produce a relationship harvest.

With the economy in a slump, many business people are desperate for sales, and because of that are not looking at the long term. They don't want to invest any time into getting to know the other person. They want to make a sale, and move on. That is the OLD way.

To be successful now, you must strive to connect in a meaningful way, and then stay connected. In the past, it may have been sufficient to keep in touch with business contacts for a few years, and if they moved on to another business, decide then whether it was worthwhile to continue to maintain connection.

Now, the majority of business people do not stay static in one position or with one company for very long. And you may not, either. As you build your network, both personally and professionally, think of it as an important personal asset. You want to be able to take it with you, no matter what you are doing, or where your career takes you.

In my career, I have had a solo medical practice, been faculty at multiple locations, moved into the private not-for-profit area, and then into my own business. I have lived in Missouri, Illinois, and Southern California. In all the moves, I have carried my contacts with me.

Another aspect of connection that has altered how we stay in touch is the broad use of social media. If we consider that digital connection has only been available for a few years, it is impossible to foresee what may be coming. Maybe it falls within the range of science fiction.

Not too long ago, the only mobile communication devices were those seen on Star Trek. Now we carry a device with us everywhere that is a small computer masquerading as a phone. Google Glass and Apple watches have been developed, although most people are still just using mobile phones. And instant video communication has become commonplace. No matter where you are in the world, you can potentially see and hear someone on your smartphone who can be anywhere with a mobile phone connection.

Most business people are using a variety of social media platforms, but they may not be working as well as they hope to stay front of mind with prospects, customers and clients. For example, it is not sufficient to merely post on Facebook or Twitter. You also need to be able to respond to postings that are directed to you. For example, I have been able to establish a relationship with an author I first started following on Twitter, because whenever I would repost or comment on his posts, he would respond to me.

Then I started following him on Facebook, and the same thing happened. I feel connected to him, even though we have never met in person. And I have purchased two of his books, even though they are not within a genre I normally read.

On the other hand, when I tried to introduce two people I knew on Twitter to each other, and one of them never acknowledged the interaction, I didn't try again. Behavior that is not rewarded tends to extinguish on its own. To get people to continue to interact with you, you need to make sure you are responding to them online.

The downside to all the posting people are doing on Facebook and LinkedIn is that only a small percentage of their connections will see their postings. It all depends on the algorithm de jour being employed by the platform at the time. And that is a moving target. Over and over I see "experts" advising on how to get more of your target market to see your postings. I am not convinced.

People want to make more of a personal connection. That is what has spurred the growth of YouTube and Vimeo. We want to know people better than what we can through email or texting. With live video, not only do you see the person live, it is interactive. Whether you are doing YouTube or Facebook Live, you can find people in all parts of the world who are interested in the same things you are.

The trick to using all types of social media is to create a connection that persists. How do we get beyond just saying "hi"? How do we maintain connections long enough that they will lead to business?

At the beginning of this book, I asked you to imagine yourself meeting people at a networking event, and then evaluating what you do with those business cards. You were asked to look at your current system of follow-up. That was your OLD way of doing business.

Then I urged you to consider a NEW way, thinking long term, and using a system for strategic follow-up. Now you can imagine a different way, a less stressful way of following up, not just with potential customers and clients, but also with people you meet along the way, who you want to include long term in your network.

When you think long term, you are more strategic in the way you pursue your business. You look at how you can help other people, and stay connected with people you like, just because you have rapport with them. You think about what you can do for people you meet, not just what they can do for you. You don't follow up with everyone you meet, because you understand not everyone is a good fit for you and your business. You let people know you appreciate them as part of your follow-up plan. You are creating an asset you can own for the lifetime of your career. Cherish it.

Elmer Wheeler advocated practicing appreciation as a way to overcome shyness and self-consciousness. When you focus on how you can show others how much you appreciate what they do for you, it helps you shift your focus outward, rather than focusing inward worrying about what people think about you. He advises you to catch people doing things that you can thank them for. He says to show appreciation because:

- It is the easiest way known to get along with people.

- It makes people glad to do things for you.

- It is a sure-fire formula to overcome timidity and to become popular with people.

Remember to tell everyone thank you over and over again. Appreciation will endear you to others, and ensure they will remember you when they need your service. I just saw another posting by Bob Burg on Facebook about the need to send thank you cards. He said:

When speaking about this during sales and leadership conferences I'll often hear from successful audience members who do this regularly. One of the most common stories is their discovering that many of those to whom they've sent these notes... have kept them!

Yes, people often keep them! Why?

Because...

1. they've been acknowledged;

2. they've been acknowledged in a powerful and personal way;

3. they received something from you they most likely have never received before.

In his excellent book, Creating Magic (highly recommended!!) former Executive Vice President of Operations for the Walt Disney World® Resort, Lee Cockerell — an avid note writer — shared a very touching story of a team member who had his note framed...and hung in his home!

Someone posted in response:

I have found customers are more likely to refer you more too. Each thank you note has generally netted me one referral almost immediately, and almost 8 over the course of a year. All, because I took time to acknowledge, and say Thank you.

As always, I remain a fan of sending thank you cards as part of keeping in touch with customers. Every November, the month we celebrate Thanksgiving, I send at least one gratitude card a day to people who come to mind who could benefit from knowing that I am thinking about them, and care about them.

I sent a gratitude card to a friend who runs a charity for cancer patients and their families, *UCAAN.org*. In it, I told her all the reasons I appreciated her and what she did. She posted pictures of it on Facebook with this comment: *"Thank you Kaaren Douglas for being an amazing friend and an awesome supporter!! This card made me cry!"*

Who could you tell today how much they mean to you? Don't just think about them; let them know how you feel. You will be contributing to a happier and better place for everyone.

Appendix

Marketing Profile

Name: _____

Cell: _____

BDay:_____

Business: _____

Title: _____

Mailing Address _____

How did you get started?

What do you like most about your business?

How are you different?

What are other people in your industry doing to find and get customers?

What are your goals?

What is the value of a lifelong customer?

What does it cost to move people from contacts to raving fans?

How are you currently marketing your business?

What follow-up systems do you have in place?

Walk me through the follow-up process you use after you make contact for the first time.

How do you prepare and plan for a networking event?

How do you categorize your contacts when you first meet them?

List the groups you put contacts in for follow-up. What kind of contact management program are you using?

How soon after you meet someone do you contact them?

What is your preferred method of contact?

Do you ask your contacts what their preferred method of contact is? (Txt, email, FB, LI, YouTube, Pinterest, fax, phone, regular mail)

How do you thank your contacts?

How do you ask your contacts and customers if you can send them a newsletter or link to your blog?

What kind of loyalty program or discounts are you currently offering?

What kind of free report or other free product/premium are you offering your contacts if they go to your website and give you their contact information?

What is the response rate – how many people usually take action?

How often do you send some new information to your contacts to get more information from them or to offer another product?

Resources:

Articles

1. Oldroyd, JB, K McElheran and D Elkington, *Harvard Business Review* 3/20/2011: The Short Life of Online Sales Leads

2. Robertson, K, *About.com*, 12/15/2014: The Power of Follow Up. Say what you're going to do and then do it.

3. Zetlin, M, *Inc.com*, 3/6/2014: The Art of Following Up (Without Being Annoying)

4. Frey, D, *BusinessKnowHow.com*, 2003: Follow-Up Marketing: How to Win More Sales with Less Effort

5. Clay, R, *MarketingDonut.co.uk*, 2013: Why 8% of sales people get 80% of sales

6. Chu, X, *Ezinearticles.co*m, 12/10/2009: How Many Times Should You Follow Up Before Giving Up Your Insurance Prospects?

7. Underkofler, A, *Followupsuccess.com*, 7/31/2009: Creating a Follow Up Strategy

8. Underkofler, A, *Followupsuccess.com*, 4/28/2009: Creating Great Follow Up with Your Clients in 7 Simple Steps

9. Underkofler, A, *Followupsuccess.com*, 7/31/2012: Surprising Statistics Showing Why Your Customers Stop Buying

10. Callier, H, *Yourmoneyisinthefollowup.com*, 12/31/2012: Systematized Follow Up

11. Moltz, B, *Smallbiztrends.com*, 10/8/2013: 7 Ways to Master the Art of Customer Follow Up,

12. Britton, S, *Life-longlearner.com*, 2013: How to Write an Effective Follow Up Email

13. Sales Follow Up Call | Tips and Techniques at *Hubpages.com*, 6/9/2010.

14. How to Follow Up With Customers at *MoreBusiness.com*, 3/2/2009

15. Fenn, D, *Inc.com*, 8/31/2010: 10 Ways to Get More SalesFrom Existing Customers

16. Hornor, J, *Canadaone.com*, 12/31/2000: EffectiveFollow-up Will Make Your Sales Soar

17. Williams, D, *Ezinearticles.com*, 1/13/2008: After SaleCustomer Follow-Up Tips18. How To Turn New Customers Into Repeat Customers (Customer Loyalty Secrets) by Derek Halpern

18. Halpern, D, *Socialtriggers.com*, How to Turn New Customers Into Repeat Customers (customer loyalty secrets) by Derek Halpern

19. Nunes, Joseph and Dreze, Xavier, *The Endowed Progress Effect: How Artificial Advancement Increases Effort*. Journal of Consumer Research, Vol. 32, March 2006. Available at SSRN: *http://papers.ssrn.com/sol3/papers.cfm?abstract_id=991962*

20. Hayden, CJ, *Businessknowhow.co*m, 7 Easy Steps to Follow Up by Phone

21. Burg, B, *Burg.com*, 11/23/2015: The Gratitude Tool That Works Every Time

22. Direct Mail Effectiveness Statistics by The Direct Mail Association, *Yourbusiness.azcentral.com*

Books

1. Adler, Jordan: *Beach Money.* An easy read from the perspective of someone who tried a series of network marketing companies before he found his home. Lots of insight about the need to keep going.

2. Burg, Bob: *Endless Referrals.* The first book I read when I started networking for my business. Lots of great tips for how to follow up using a personal touch.

3. Burg, Bob and John David Mann: *Go-Givers Sell More.* The authors propose an approach that may NOT be intuitive: Create value for others, and you will be more successful at sales.

4. Comm, Joel, Dave Taylor, Guy Kawasaki: *Twitter Power 3.0. How to Dominate Your Market One Tweet at a Time*. If you are not a Twitter power user, and want some good tips on how to use Twitter for marketing your business, this is a good place to start.

5. Duhigg, Charles: *The Power of Habit*. This book explains how habits are formed, and what you need to do to use that to your advantage.

6. Eker, T. Harv: *Secrets of the Millionaire Mind*. Eker provides information about how you may be your own worst enemy. I found it so powerful I did attend two seminars put on by his company.

7. Fiore, Neil: *The Now Habit at Work*. A helpful guide to why we procrastinate, and how to move beyond it.

8. Gladwell, Malcolm: *The Tipping Point*. This book gave me a lot of insight about how I think, and what it takes to be a successful networker. Unfortunately, for many, it is challenging to learn, because it is not intuitive to them.

9. Gladwell, Malcolm: *Blink. The Power of Thinking Without Thinking*. An exploration of how to weigh the advantages and disadvantages of leaping to conclusions based on snap judgements.

10. Godin, Seth: *Permission Marketing*. An easy and simple explanation of the difference between getting people to express an interest in whatever you are selling, and how that is more successful long term than just blasting away with no thought to who your customer really is.

11. Haaz, Carol: *Don't Be a Secret Agent.* The author takes you through a systematic approach to marketing your small business. Although she is approaching it from the point of view of a realtor, the overall message still applies.

12. Lederman, Michelle Tillis: *The 11 Laws of Likability.* If you want to be more successful at networking, think long term, and do the best you can to develop truly lasting relationships.

13. Lofholm, Eric and Judy O'Higgins: *Duplication.* Basic book on how to be better at building your network marketing team.

14. Mackay, Harvey: *The Mackay MBA of Selling in the Real World.* Quick lessons that teach the essentials of selling.

15. McKay, Harvey: *Dig Your Well Before You're Thirsty.* McKay lays out why it is so essential to keep following up with your contacts, and think long term.

16. Nirenberg, Andrea: *Nonstop Networking.* Focuses on the need for building mutually beneficial relationships.

17. Prodromou, Ted: *Ultimate Guide to LinkedIn for Business, Second Edition.* Helpful guide to help you use LinkedIn more effectively for business.

18. Schreves, Ric and Michelle Krasniak: *Social Media Optimization for Dummies.* Helpful guide to using social media to direct traffic to your website, and interact effectively with people and get the followers you want.

19. Sheldon, Betsy and Joyce Hadley: *The Smart Woman's Guide to Networking*. This guide discusses the reasons why networking is a skill that is a necessity for business women.

20. Sweeney, Joe: *Networking is a Contact Sport*. Focus on what you can give to the people you meet. Felt his advice about follow up was a little over the top.

21. Wheeler, Elmer: *How to Sell Yourself to Others*. First published in 1977, this book gives tips along the line of Dale Carnegie's many books, from the perspective of a successful salesman.

22. Wyatt, Tommy and Curtis Lewsey: *Appreciation Marketing*. Easily readable guide to using appreciation, rather than promotion to grow your business.

23. Yarnell, Mark and Rene Reid Yarnell: *Your First Year in Network Marketing. Overcome Your Fears, Experience Success, and Achieve Your Dreams!* A great starter book, with basic information, for someone who wants to build a network marketing business.

Expert Advisors

1. Neil Palache, The Wealth Creator Company for Women, http://www.thewealthcreatorcompany.com

2. Michael Weissenborn, https://www.linkedin.com/pub/michael-weissenborn/28/162/223

3. Eric Lofholm, http://www.saleschampion.com/eric-lofholm/

4. Todd Falcone, http://www.toddfalcone.com

5. Casey Eberhart, htttp://www.theidealnetworkinger.com

6. Roberta Nadler, http://www.connectthedotsadvertising.com/

Online Resources

1. *Yelp.com* Write reviews, and find reviews on different types of businesses.

2. *www.kaarendouglas.biz*: Contact Manager allows you to track your contacts and send cards. You can upload contacts from Outlook or other CRM systems.

3. Worthwhile Referral Services: *http://worthwhilereferralsources.com/*

4. *Meetup.com*: Site for meetings of various kinds.

5. Auto Desk with writing surface: AutoDesk at Office World

6. EdgeUp Network: Learn more about Social Sync for LinkedIn

7. LinkedIn: *www.linkedin.com/in/kaarendouglas*

8. FaceBook: *https://www.facebook.com/DouglasMarketingConcepts*

9. Google+: *https://plus.google.com/u/0/+KaarenDouglas*

10. Twitter: *@douglasmkting*

Cell Phone Applications

ScanBizCards: *https://www.circleback.com/scanbizcards*

This is the cell phone application I use to scan business cards immediately after I meet a contact at a networking event. Don't bother with the free version, because you want to be able to save all the cards and sync them with the cloud version of this app.

Camcard: *https://www.camcard.com/*

A contact recommended this app for the iPhone. You can export contacts to a CRM, including Salesforce, SugarCRM or an Excel spreadsheet.

Evernote: *https://evernote.com*

An app with free and premium versions.

Online Tools

CMap Program: *http://cmap.ihmc.us/*

Yesware: *http://www.yesware.com/*

A plugin available for Gmail and Outlook. There is a free and premium version. Use it to see when your emails are opened.

Constant Contact: *http://www.constantcontact.com/*

Email marketing tool.

Mail Chimp: *http://mailchimp.com/*

Email marketing tool. Free version available.

AWeber: *http://www.aweber.com/*

Email marketing tool. Cell phone app available.

Form to Call: *https://www.formtocall.org/*

Instant lead contact system, to make it possible to immediately contact someone looking at your website.

STRATEGIC FOLLOW UP

About the Author

 **Kaaren Douglas, MD, MSPH** had a solo family practice, and then completed a Robert Wood Johnson fellowship emphasizing research and teaching skills. She enjoyed an academic career at the University of Missouri-Kansas City, and the University of California-Irvine. While at UCI she completed a Management Development Program in Health Care to enhance her management skills.

Leaving academia, Dr. Douglas became the Director of Geriatric Programs at the Motion Picture and Television Fund (MPTF). She also became a Board Member of the Southern California Cancer Pain Initiative, inspired by her desire to assist her husband when he was diagnosed with cancer. After his passing, she decided to branch out from medicine, and discovered an interest and passion for entrepreneurial pursuits. Her experiences as teacher/clinician and manager are assets in helping her guide other entrepreneurs to be more effective in their own businesses.

Dr. Douglas has served as a consultant to multiple academic institutions and national agencies, including the Senior Citizen Advisory Committee for U.S. Representative Lynn Martin. She is the author of *A Practical Guide to Clinical Teaching in Medicine,* as well as numerous scientific and research publications.

As a business owner, she received commendations from the City and County of Los Angeles for her service as a Director of the Chatsworth/Porter Ranch Chamber of Commerce 2010–2011. Currently, she serves as an Entre Leader for Bring It, a Mastermind Group sponsored by the United States Business Bureau.

How to Connect with Dr. Kaaren

Dr. Kaaren Douglas, The Follow Up Doctor helps you develop your own system of follow up in many ways:

- Individual mentoring

- Workshops for networking groups, businesses, organizations

- Speaking engagements, topics including:
  - *How to Use Your Cell Phone to Follow Up on the Spot*
  - *Use Long Term Follow-Up to Create Raving Fans*

The New Way to Build Relationships Using Social Media

- Online at *KaarenDouglas.Biz*

- Blog posts at *TheFollowUpDoctor.com*

- *Facebook.com/douglasmarketingconcepts*

- *Twitter.com/douglasmkting*

- *Linkedin.com/in/kaarendouglas*

- *Pinterest/drkaaren*

Dr. Kaaren can be contacted at *drkaaren@thefollowupdoctor.com*

Made in the USA
Charleston, SC
17 January 2017